Watching Grandma
Circle the Drain

Watching Grandma Circle the Drain

Allen Smith

Edited by Tim Hunter

authorHOUSE®

AuthorHouse™
1663 Liberty Drive
Bloomington, IN 47403
www.authorhouse.com
Phone: 1-800-839-8640

First published by AuthorHouse   07/23/2011

ISBN: 978-1-4634-3793-0 (sc)
ISBN: 978-1-4634-3792-3 (ebk)

Library of Congress Control Number: 2011912608

Printed in the United States of America

Any people depicted in stock imagery provided by Thinkstock are models, and such images are being used for illustrative purposes only.
Certain stock imagery © Thinkstock.

This book is printed on acid-free paper.

Because of the dynamic nature of the Internet, any web addresses or links contained in this book may have changed since publication and may no longer be valid. The views expressed in this work are solely those of the author and do not necessarily reflect the views of the publisher, and the publisher hereby disclaims any responsibility for them.

Contents

Introduction

I love to write. And, although I've written different types of work throughout most of my life, it wasn't until after publishing my master's thesis that I really got bitten by the writer's bug. I should have known something was wrong. Anyone who thoroughly enjoys writing a book titled, "The Relationship Between Glycosylated Hemoglobin and Plasma Lactate Accumulation During Sub-maximal Exercise in the Type II Diabetic" must have a screw loose. The unfortunate result was a 320 page behemoth filled with charts, graphs, scattergrams and tons of medical terminology that no one has read since the day it was slid onto the library shelf. It hasn't been turned into a Broadway Musical and to date, no major studio has asked me for the rights to make it into an Academy Award winning motion picture—although I do stay up nights rehearsing my acceptance speech after Sandra Bullock hands me my Oscar for Best Picture in a Biochemical Comedy.

Since then, I've written thousands of different types of articles—mostly about how to get through life—from my twisted perspective. And twisted, it is. In **Watching Grandma Circle the Drain**, I wrote, "On Becoming a Famous Writer," a fictitious, overstuffed narrative of what it's like to become an award winning writer. Although I have won awards, I'm still not famous yet—but I have a pretty good idea about how to get there. One of the secrets I share is to constantly be on the lookout for your most fertile writing venues. For me, it's the shower. I don't know why, but every time I get a really good idea for a story, it's in the shower. As a result, I've become a very CLEAN writer.

I tend to write a lot about fantasy. Not of pirate ships, flying elephants or magic squirrels, but of things that could easily go awry in the normal course of life. While reading the newspaper, a book or watching the news on television, I amuse myself by listening to stories and imagining what

1

would happen if the boundaries were taken away from traditional stories. Instead of a terrorist smuggling plastic explosives aboard an airliner (like we've all become accustomed to reading), what if it was a "sticky bomb" made from Mentos candy mints and a liter of Diet Coke? Hence, the piece, "Sticky Bomb Threat Foiled."

The first part of this book is a collection of stories and entertaining pieces you might be familiar with. In "Where the Sun Don't Shine," I write about the thrill of participating in an adult right of passage—my first sigmoidoscopy. Another popular subject I like to explore is something I know absolutely nothing about: dating—specifically on-line dating and how men and women get together has changed over the years. In "Expelled from Match.com" I recount the true story of how the famous dating service tossed me out of their dating pool—not once, but three times—for pushing the envelope too far. Other pieces like "The Great Sperm Audition," "Customs, Laws and Faux Pas" and "Hypochondriacs Make Me Sick" were written solely to entertain and after having read them, leave you a better person—well, maybe not better, but at least, more informed.

The second part of the book is titled, "Ripped from the Headlines," and parodies some of the hottest topics of the day, in news format. Nothing is sacred. In "For Better or For Worse," a 31-year-old man abandons traditional dating practices and decides to become the first person on record to marry himself. This is followed 18 months later by his unfortunate divorce in, "The End of a Love Affair." Later, the biggest disaster since the Hindenburg explosion of 1937 is chronicled in "The Great Soufflé Explosion" and occurs in a Lakehurst, New Jersey kitchen on the anniversary of the sad event when a lighter than air dessert goes up in flames. In sports, the entire world of professional cycling is put on its ear, when officials allow women to compete in the Tour de France—and a 21-year-old female law student from Long Island, New York wins! Then, a 13-year-old boy gets busted for taking performance enhancing drugs in, "Steroids Invade the World of Professional Chess." As you can see, nothing is sacred once it creeps into my consciousness.

One of the advantages of being a comedy writer is you can write about anything you like—little or none of it has to be true—as long as it's believable and it gets a laugh. When you put that together with real life events, it's a formula for disaster—or success, depending on how you choose to interpret it.

If you're looking for something inspirational and educational—something you can share with young children, this is not the book for you. But, if you're looking for a way to take a 15-minute vacation from reality, you've come to the right place. I hope you enjoy reading the stories in this book as much as I have writing them and that you'll recommend **Watching Grandma Circle the Drain** to your friends. We could all use a good laugh.

Allen Smith

Me No Speak Good Mexican

I've lived in the western United States for over 50 years and have somehow managed to escape learning Spanish the entire time. It's not that I haven't tried. I took 4 years of it in college. But repeating lines out of my workbook like, "Maria está viendo la televisión en la casa." ("Maria is watching television in the house") didn't seem to be nearly as useful as phrases like, "Quisiera mirar abajo la blusa de esa muchacha." ("I'd like to look down that girl's blouse.") When I started teaching skiing to visitors from Mexico City, I found that it might even save someone's life. While watching one of my students careening down the mountain at mach 6 on skis, it's important to know how to say, "¡Pare o usted se estrellará y matarse con ese cuarto de baño en el aire libre!" ("Stop or you'll crash into that outhouse and kill yourself!")

Anyone who speaks a foreign language will tell you the best way to become fluent is to totally immerse yourself in the culture. By fumbling over the simplest words like milk, sugar, bread, sex, hashish, irritable bowel syndrome, unwanted pregnancy and federal penitentiary, you quickly become absorbed in not only the vocabulary and sentence structure but also how the language is used in the context of every day living. So, in 1972 I packed up my VW bus and headed down to 'ol Mexico to learn how to speak Spanish.

Fortunately, I had friends of some friends of some friends of a family who lived in Guadalajara that were willing to take me under their wing. The first evening after I arrived, I met the Pintados at an upscale restaurant in town called, "El Pescado de Ahogamiento" (The Drowning Fish)—a popular destination by locals because of its remarkable seafood. After introductions all around, the waiter came to take our orders. Señor Pintado started by asking the waiter, "¿Que tiene en el menu que no me haga daño?" or "What do you have on the menu that won't make me sick?" A good phrase to know when dining out. I scrawled that down in my notebook. His wife Isabel and their 15 daughters, Juliana, Marisol, Evita, Esperanza, Mercedes, Jacinta, Paloma, Daniela, Ella, Carlota, Allegra, Tia, Daniela, Adriana and Gabriella gave the waiter their orders and then looked at me. Since it didn't matter if the menu was upside down or not, I pointed to something I vaguely remembered seeing at Chili's.

While we were waiting for our orders to arrive, Señor Pintado and I attempted to stumble through an adult conversation using simple words, our hands, feet, silverware and any other object that would make up for this gringo's failure to understand even the simplest Spanish terms.

It's incredibly frustrating when you'd like to say, "When do you think the middle class will see signs of improvement in the economic slowdown?" but instead you inadvertently come out with something like, "Can I put my suitcase in your virgin daughter's ear?"

After dinner, Señor Pintado explained that if I was going to languish in the luxury of his comfortable hacienda, I would be expected to pull my own weight. So, through one of his business acquaintances he arranged a job for me moving furniture. He said that it would be a good way for me to learn about the Mexican culture and improve my Spanish while keeping me away from his beautiful daughters Juliana, Marisol, Evita, Esperanza, Mercedes, Jacinta, Paloma, Daniela, Ella, Carlota, Allegra, Tia, Daniela, Adriana and Gabriella. I started the next morning.

Around 9:00, a badly beaten moving truck arrived at our front door, engulfed in a cloud of exhaust and flames. Julio, my "compañero de trabajo" (co-worker), slithered out from behind the wheel and exchanged niceties with Señor Pintado before stuffing me into the back of the truck. Our first stop was a warehouse where we transferred 30 or 40 extremely heavy bed frames, sofas, dressers, tables and armoires to our truck before making our first stop. Anxious to begin learning my new language, I started reading the packing labels on the boxes and mattresses: "¡Advertencia! ¡No quite del colchón ni intente tragar!" ("Warning! Do not remove from mattress or attempt to swallow!") and, "¡Extremadamente pesado! ¡No intente moverse sin una carretilla elevadora!" ("Extremely heavy! Do not attempt to move without a forklift!"). These were very useful phrases but a bit unsettling since there were only the two of us.

My next chance to put my Spanish to work was being the bottom man on an 8 foot sofa as we wrestled it up 10 flights of stairs. Muscling heavy furniture through tight spaces afforded me a genuine opportunity to use the language in the manner in which it was meant to be spoken. For instance, I learned that "¡Empuje más difícilmente, usted grasa, bastardo perezoso!" meant, "Push harder, you fat, lazy bastard!" and "¡Parada! ¡Usted aplastó mi pulgar en la pared!" is loosely translated to "Stop! You squashed my thumb into the wall!" Good to know.

After we finished our shift, Julio was kind enough to drop me off in front of the flea-bitten motel room Señor Pintado had rented for me to keep me away from his beautiful daughters Juliana, Marisol, Evita, Esperanza, Mercedes, Jacinta, Paloma, Daniela, Ella, Carlota, Allegra, Tia, Daniela, Adriana and Gabriella. After a quick shower and a reheated plate of leftover eel intestines from last night's dinner, I settled in for a night of television. Since remote controls hadn't yet made their way to the Archeluta Motel, I had to crouch in front of the set, flicking the dial between commercials I couldn't understand and re-runs of popular American television series from the 1960s. I finally landed on a re-run of "Hawaii Five-O"—in Spanish, naturally. You haven't lived until you've heard Steve McGarrett barking orders at Dann-o in Spanish. "¡Llegue ese cuerpo al depósito de cadavers!" said McGarrett ("Get that body to the morgue!") "¡El practicar surf que va de me!" ("I'm going surfing!") It is, however, a good way to learn Spanish.

I persevered as long as I could as Julio's apprentice but ultimately decided that there must be easier ways to learn how to speak the language. So, I bid adieu to Señor and Señora Pintado and his beautiful daughters Juliana, Marisol, Evita, Esperanza, Mercedes, Jacinta, Paloma, Daniela, Ella, Carlota, Allegra, Tia, Daniela, Adriana and Gabriella. I returned home after a month in Mexico and enrolled in a night school class that promised to have me speaking fluent Spanish in just 12 weeks. ¡Qué bueno!

The class was made up of 12 students—3 guys from the Middle East, 2 from France, 3 Czechs, 1 German, 2 Russians—and me—the only

American. The only thing that we had in common was that none of us knew how to speak a lick of Spanish, so we were all on common ground.

When American schools teach Spanish in the United States, they start slowly to get you thinking that you can actually learn the language and then go in for the kill. After 2 weeks of simple sentences like, "Maria tiene gusto de comer la cena en el cuarto de baño." ("Maria likes to eat dinner in the bathroom.") the teacher brought us to our knees by making us conjugate the tenses of "echar un pedo"—to fart: I fart, you fart, he farts, we fart and they fart. Then, she moved on to the 7 simple present and 7 compound tenses: the present indicative, imperfect indicative, preterit, future, simple potential, present subjunctive, imperfect subjunctive, perfect indicative, pluperfect indicative, previous preterit, future perfect, compound potential, perfect subjunctive, imperfect subjunctive and the imperative. It's important that you master these tenses so that you can properly say, "I fart, you fart, he/she/it farts, we fart, they fart, I farted, you farted, he/she/it farted, we farted, they farted, I am farting, you are farting, he/she/it is farting, they are farting, I was farting, I had farted, I had been farting, I will have been farting and I will have farted."

By the time the semester was over, my head was swimming and I still couldn't carry on a conversation with any of the dishwashers at my uncle's restaurant. I felt doomed to another year of screaming and waving my ski poles at my students while they continued ricocheting off the snow fences and other students in class, "¡Pare o usted se estrellará y matarse con ese cuarto de baño en el aire libre!"

I still can't speak Spanish.

Instructions 101

For the past year and a half, I've woken up to a familiar greeting from my digital alarm clock. 12:00 12:00 12:00 12:00 12:00. Ever since the power went out, my alarm clock has been winking at me, hoping that one day, I'll learn how to set its time. Fat chance.

So, one evening last week, I dragged out the user manual to try to figure out how to change the time from 12:00 midnight to the correct time of the day—which, as luck would have it was 12:00 midnight. Like most user manuals, the 64 page instruction guide is broken down into separate language sections for French, Spanish, Yiddish, Lithuanian, Tagalog, Japanese, Chinese, German, Icelandic, Norwegian, Danish and Bulgarian. Flip it over and you'll find Dutch, Arabic, Portuguese, Farsi, Vietnamese, Turkish, Korean, Italian, Thai, Cantonese, Polish, Burmese and even a section devoted to Pig Latin. Thankfully, the last page was written in English.

Due to the litigious nature of our society, I find consumer instructions and warnings on everything I use. But because of the way the instructions are written, they're almost impossible to interpret. Instead of clear sentences that tell you how to use a product, you'll find a series of pictures (with no words) and an 800 telephone number to somewhere halfway around the world. There's a diagram with one end of a cord going from the S-video output on the DVD player to the input on the microwave oven, followed by three color-coded RCA plugs pointing to the red, yellow and white audio inputs on the toaster. Somewhere in the instructions, you'll find the obligatory illustration of a human finger poking an electrical outlet with a large, red international circle with a line through it, suggesting that you shouldn't test the electricity with your index finger. With that, the manufacturer is off the hook.

While brushing my teeth the next morning, I noticed for the first time that there were explicit directions on the side of the toothpaste tube on how to safely brush your teeth, with a list of all its side effects. I've been brushing my teeth all my life and never once felt compelled to stop and read the directions—but they're there, so I guess I should start reading them.

Later, I started to wonder about all of the other directions I've glossed over all these years and made a promise to myself that I was going to start following them. Here's just a few:

Mitchum Antiperspirant: Remove the cap from the top of the product and twist the knob at the bottom of the container, counter clockwise until the product begins to ooze from the small pores at the top of the dispenser. While holding the dispenser in your right hand, lift your left elbow away from your body until your upper arm is parallel to the floor. Point the tip of the dispenser toward your underarm at a 45-degree angle where your upper arm and torso meet (armpit). Press the dispenser lightly against your skin while dragging the applicator down, applying a thin film of product onto your skin. Repeat under the other arm. Vigorously flap your upper arms up and down to dry the product before donning your shirt or blouse. *Warning:* discontinue use if you develop blue vision, oily stools, bleeding nipples, black tongue disease, amnesia, tricholtillomania or rectal bleeding.

Scope Mouthwash: Grasp the middle of the bottle firmly with your right hand, while squeezing and turning the bottle top counter clockwise. Pour 2-3 ounces of mouthwash into a small glass and secure the cap back onto the bottle. Open your mouth approximately halfway and pour the mouthwash into your mouth. Close your lips, making a tight seal and gently inflate your cheeks to approximately 20 pounds per square inch (PSI). Quickly reverse the pressure to approximately—10 PSI. Repeat the process 5 to 6 times. Bend forward at your waist positioning your head directly over your bathroom sink. Open your mouth and expel the mouthwash into sink. Return to a normal standing position. *Warning:* Do not use as radiator anti-freeze or to irrigate your eyes. Keep product out of reach of teen-age boys younger than drinking age. Discontinue use if you begin to experience hallucinations, severe acne, uncontrolled flatulence, limb spasticity, Grocer's Itch or prolonged hiccups.

Kleenex Tissue: Using the tips of your thumb and index finger, gently pull one tissue from the top of the container. After folding the tissue in half, cradle it between the tips of your fingers inside the palm of your hand. Inhale deeply through the nose and hold. Bring the tissue towards the outside of the nostrils of your nose and gently pinch your fingers against the outside surface of your nose. After closing your mouth and epiglottis, rapidly exhale the inner contents of your nose into the tissue at a pressure not to exceed 35 PSI. Repeat several times, taking care to suppress any audible noises. While pinching the sides of your nostrils with the tissue, gently pull away from your nostrils. *Warning*: Exceeding 75 PSI may result in spontaneous pneumothorax of the vestibular canals (blowing out your eardrums). Do not attempt procedure while driving, text messaging, eating hot soup or meeting your in-laws for the first time. Discontinue and seek medical attention if you notice brain matter on the tissue, contract Elephantitis, Werewolf Syndrome, Pica, Blaschko's Lines or Jumping Frenchman Disorder.

Angel Soft Toilet Paper: Locate the last square of paper at end of the toilet paper roll; depending on the type of dispenser installation, the last sheet may be either on the top or underneath the roll. Firmly grasp the end of the roll with the tip of your index finger and thumb. Using either an underhand or overhand technique is acceptable. Gently pull the paper away from the roll until four or five squares have cleared the roll. Quickly snap the end of the paper to tear it from the remainder of the roll while supporting the roll with your other hand. Fold the length of the toilet paper over itself to create a pad over the tips of your fingers, anchoring the paper between your fingers. Using a free hand, pull one gluteal cheek away from the center line of your body, creating a wide crevice. Beginning midway down the crevice, gently swab the pad of toilet paper across your rectum using moderate pressure of approximately 20 Pascal (where 1 atm = 1.013×105 Pa = 101.3 kPa). Deposit the used paper in the toilet bowl. Repeat several times until the area is clean. *Warning*: Do not loan used toilet paper to others or store in pocket or purse. Do not attempt the procedure with a wire brush, emery cloth, wax paper, sandpaper, notebook paper or the front page of the New York Times.

Wyeth Preparation H: Remove trousers, dress or underwear. From a standing position, gently bend your knees to a squatting position. Open the product tube and squeeze a one-inch line of product onto the tip of your middle finger. Using your other hand, gently pull one gluteal cheek to the side. Gently slide the finger with the product over, around and into the rectum, distributing the product in a clockwise direction. Replace the cap on the product tube and return to medicine cabinet. *Warning*: To avoid accidentally exchanging products, do not store in close proximity to tooth paste, Ben-Gay, Pep Boys Quick Lube, Leonard's Radiator Repair Paste, Fiesta's Hot Sauce, silicone tub and shower caulking or Crazy Glue.

Meanwhile, my alarm clock is still flashing 12:00 12:00 12:00 and I can't get back to sleep. In the morning, I'm going to take it back to the store—and trade it in for one with the correct time.

Expelled from Match.com!

I haven't been on a date in years. And, for good reason. By the time I endure the excruciation of the hunt, anticipation of the first date, cost of dry cleaning my best leisure suit and trying to figure out what base I'm on, it's just not worth it. It's much easier just to stay at home and pretend I'm having a good time by trolling the online dating scene and taking care of myself.

Last year I enrolled at Match.com using the pen name of "MrMarvelous" just to see if there was anyone out there as desperate as I was to meet their perfect mate. After blowing off an entire day's work perusing the women within 100 miles of my zip code, seven major metropolises and all of the neighborhoods I've ever lived, it became readily apparent that of the 40 million single men and women who subscribe to on-line dating services, most are looking for the same thing—and their profiles reflect exactly that. So, to leverage myself against my male competitors and attract more than my fair share of the lovelier sex, I decided to create the following original member profile to flaunt my rapier wit. After all, isn't that what women want: a man with a sense of humor

Dating headline:
Tom Selleck Look-a-like In Search of Love

For fun:
I enjoy interesting outdoor activities like sneaking up on bears and startling skunks. I like doing things in dark, damp places and want to find someone who enjoys the same. I love the ocean and dream of opening a five-star skin care clinic at the trendy Paranur Gandhi Leprosy Colony in Hawaii. Like my parole officer, I feel that if you find the right vocation, your job and your hobbies become one in the same.

My job:
I work as a telemarketer for a cemetery. Calling people at dinner time to discuss their immediate plans after death has helped me immensely with the online dating scene. After working at "Plots 'R Us" for six months, I've developed a thick enough skin to allow me to work through all of the hate mail and death threats that I've accumulated at Match.com.

My ethnicity:
I was born the only Jewish boy in a home full of Mormon women. Plagued by daily beatings at the hand of my 7-year old sister, I struck out on my own at the age of 43, in search of my father: the only gay Karate Instructor I've ever known. My mother told me that I was conceived in the back seat of a 1943 Peugeot station wagon on her prom night. Since that time, I've become inexplicably drawn to used car salesmen and the smell of cheap upholstery.

My religion:
I was baptized as a Buddhist, circumcised by a freelance Mohel and spent the first 10 years of my life sequestered in a Catholic confessional, so I consider myself religious but not spiritual. My sect believes in reverse re-incarnation: that mankind has already lived their best days in the distant past. Each time we are re-born, we return one rung lower on the ladder of life. Eventually, after returning enough times, we end up as a chewed piece of gum, stuck to the bottom of someone's shoe only to be scraped off on the curb.

Favorite hot spots:
I'm generally not a "club" person, but sometimes I'll dress up in my best leisure suit and go looking for Bakersfield disco clubs; pretty tough since discos went out in the 1970's. I love traveling and will often stow away in cargo containers aboard trans-pacific freighters. The accommodations aren't great but I've met a lot of wonderful people and have become fluent in 15 dialects of Tagalog.

Favorite things:
Since I've been paroled, life has been about taking advantage of all of the things I could never have while sharing a cell with three women: my own bar of soap, sharp objects, a mirror, keeping a whole pack of cigarettes

to myself, being able to fall asleep without screaming, getting stabilized on my medications, a new tattoo every week with a clean needle and unfettered access to the general public.

Last read:

Although I love to read, since the lobotomy I haven't been able to tackle anything much longer than 10 words before I start to hyperventilate. I generally stick to reading the instructions on Preparation H boxes or the restraining orders that inevitably come every week. Someday, I'd like to tackle a great American novel; something like "Curious George and the Pizza," "Is Your Mama a Llama?" or "The Frog and the Toad Are Friends."

About me and what I'm looking for:

My therapist tells me that I'm a mystery wrapped in an enema. I've been told that I'm good looking, sexy, have great legs, am fun to be with and am an exceptional wit. But that might have been just to get me to eat my peas.

I spend most of my time outdoors and love to travel. Not having a place to live will do that to you. I love exercise and enjoy a good chase from the police on a warm summer evening. My special lady has to be tall, smart, of good child-rearing stock and have wide hips as I intend to have a ten or fifteen kids once I get off of the anti-depressants.

I was raised by my grandparents: devout polygamists who practiced celibacy. My grandmothers used to tell me that I could be anything in life I wanted to be as long I made decisions with my "big" head instead of my "little" head.

I'm looking for the kind of woman who knows how to take care of me: the kind of lady who doesn't mind getting up in the middle of the night to adjust my IV drip or change my soiled diapers. I need a woman who likes to cuddle and hold me after my panic attacks. I'm a great conversationalist and most of the time I can form whole sentences despite the Thorazin. I like sitting by the fire sharing a good bottle of wine with my special lady. Over the years, I've amassed quite a collection of screw top wines from all over the world. I also like to think of myself as quite a good cook. In the Rocky Mountains, we have a lot of road kill during the spring, so I've become something of a connoisseur when it comes to preparing wild game.

They say that the majority of successful relationships begin in the workplace. Although I've had passionate relationships with the UPS driver, the Xerox repair person, three of the security guards, fourteen temps, all of the cleaning women and half of the secretaries, I still haven't found "the one." Having exhausted all of my workplace options, I'm turning to Match.com to meet that special someone.

I have exceptionally high standards with women that I allow into my life. They have to be either smart, dull, funny, lifeless, passionate, cold, humorless, wealthy, poor, athletic, sedentary, slim, fat, beautiful, plain, wealthy, broke, healthy, infirm, generous, cinchy, self-centered, old, young, well-traveled, self-absorbed or have just about any other quality that a man looks for in a woman; as long as they're alive, warm and breathing.

I'm not into games, so please do not email me or send me winks unless you enclose a minimum of 12 autographed 8 X 12, professionally prepared, high resolution color photographs, can type a minimum of 150 words per minute with 90% accuracy and you're ready to have lots of kids right away.

After submitting my member profile to Match.com, I was required to "agree" to their terms of use. The agreement is the usual legal mumbo-jumbo that cloaks their service in a thin veneer of protection against libelous statements flaunted in my member profile. It isn't until I read the fine print of the terms of agreement that I ran into problems. Match.com states:

1. You will not post on the Service, or transmit to other Members, any defamatory, inaccurate, abusive, obscene, profane, offensive, sexually oriented, threatening, harassing, racially offensive, or illegal material.
2. You will not provide inaccurate, misleading or false information to the Company or to any other Member.

3. You understand and agree that Match.com may review and delete any content, messages, double-blind emails, photos or profiles.
4. You will not impersonate any person or entity.
5. All information provided must be accurate and current.

Point two is what got me into trouble. Well, actually it was all of them

After submitting my profile, I received a computer generated email that stated:

Dear MrMarvelous,

Thank you for submitting your profile to Match.com.

Unfortunately, we are unable to approve it at this time. Please submit another profile or alter the text you previously sent by following these steps:

- All information provided must be accurate and current
- Must be in English
- You must be single or separated from your spouse
- Do not include detailed personal information (i.e.: your full name, street address, contact information, date of birth, etc.) to help protect your online anonymity
- Do not include any language which could be considered defamatory or offensive in any way (i.e.: sexually explicit, promotes racism, references to inflicting bodily harm to yourself or others, etc.)

I wouldn't have been so upset with their guidelines if I hadn't already been duped by hundreds of women who described themselves as "athletic and toned" who earn "$75,000-$150,000," "Don't smoke," only have "One or two drinks" and "Have one strategically placed tattoo." These, of course, are actually over the hill, chain-smoking, alcoholic dishrags on welfare. But, the Match.com Police don't seem to be knocking on their doors.

Once you've been expelled by Match.com, it's almost impossible to subscribe to any other on-line dating service. Word gets around fast. In my quest to find Ms. Right, I've had to resort to inventing dozens of other original screen names. But, was ultimately able to re-use my member profile.

So, the moral of the story is, "Don't mess with Match.com" or you may find yourself single for life.

Television Shows that Didn't Make the Fall Line-up

It's that time again. The time when television network executives decide which series will make their fall line-up and those that won't. Here's a brief list of what you won't be seeing on the major television networks this season:

CSI: Proctologist—CSI: Proctologist follows Dr. Sam Sloan, accompanied by hard drinking, divorced New York City Detective, Mitchell Perez through a typical work day. The opening scene shows Dr. Sloan and Detective Perez standing over a bullet-ridden body with a 12-inch Bowie knife protruding from it's back:

Detective Perez: "So, Doc. What do you think was the cause of death?"
Dr. Sloan: "It's hard to tell, Mitch. I'll have to wait until I get the body back to the lab, where I can perform a Fleets enema and a sigmoidoscopy on him. Off hand, I'm thinkin' it was polyps in his colon or extreme blood loss due to rectal fissures."

This Old Souse—After losing his major lawsuit with PBS, filing bankruptcy, divorce and hocking all of his tools to pay his alimony payments, alcoholic and drug abusing Bob Villa somehow manages to stagger around his dilapidated workshop in his stained sweatpants, showing viewers how to perform common home repairs like patching over bullet holes from the party last night, getting difficult blood stains out of carpets and replacing a front door that was run down by a Harley Davidson.

America Ain't Got Talent—Aimed at spotlighting the little guy, the judges of America Ain't Got Talent, Piers Morgan, Sharon Osbourne and Howie Mandel scoop up the leftovers from the past three seasons, looking for the absolute worst acts on stage. The winning performer (which is actually the losing performer) will get an opportunity to tour nursing homes and Veterans Administration Hospitals in southeast Florida.

Law and Order: Special Janitorial Unit—The most recent in a string of successful Law and Order programs created by Dick Wolfe, Law and Order SJU keeps viewers riveted to the edge of their seats as they follow janitors emptying trash cans, mopping up puke from holding cells, washing the detective's coffee cups and replacing the toilet paper in the women's restroom.

NCIS: Guthrie, Oklahoma—the Naval Criminal Investigation Service is challenged in a series of investigations that occur thousands of miles away from the nearest body of salt water or Naval facility. In the opening episode, the team is dispatched to Okie Ink, where sailors on leave are attempting to finagle free tattoos from owners Frankie Heller, Fenecia Doolin and Becky Burton. The sailors tell the owners that they were just trying to get the free artwork advertised in the Guthrie News Leader. After their arrests, the sailors were bussed back to Treasure Island, California where they were given dishonorable discharges and a gift book of temporary tattoos.

Lost Springs Medical—Lost Springs Medical follows three newly graduated medical students as they meander their way through their first year of residency in Wyoming's smallest town (population: 10). Students take turns barking orders at each other as they pretend to be the Chief Medical Examiner, Chief of Surgery and Chief of Emergency Medicine, performing unnecessary medical procedures on unsuspecting hitchhikers who wander into town.

Dancing with the Homeless—A spin-off of the popular reality show, Dancing with the Stars, the DWTH judges Bruno, Carrie Ann and Len evaluate the soiled, bug-infested costumes and dancing skills of homeless people at the Union Rescue Mission and on the corners of 5th and San Pedro Streets. Contestants compete for warm meals, clothes and prime sleeping locations under bridges and at the Old Greyhound Bus Terminal.

Lost: The Sahara Desert—In the latest installment of the popular adventure series, the participants are dropped from a helicopter into the complex sand dunes of Sahara Marzup, Libya and forced to duke it out against their fellow contestants, using only a piece of string, one liter of water, an iPod and a pogo stick until they reach the seacoast ports of Shott el Jerid (North Africa's largest salt lake), the Barchan Sand Dunes or the Suez Canal. From there, contestants have to swim back to the United States, where they'll compete for new visitor visas.

The Warehouse—With the failing economy at Dunder-Mifflin paper company, Michael Scott, Dwight Schrute and Pam Beesly have been demoted to the company's warehouse where they get involved in a series of hilarious circumstances like learning how to drive a fork lift, weighing boxes in shipping and receiving and figuring out how to use the time clock.

Owego Legal—The latest casualty in legal dramas has been Owego Legal. Owego is a small village in Tioga County, New York, with only 3911 permanent residents. Writer/Producer David E. Kelley said that even though he managed to land top notch talent from his previous productions, there just wasn't enough going on in the town to come up with 13 episodes worth writing about. "After covering the obituaries and the classified ads," said Kelley, "the only thing worth writing about was a man yelling obscenities at several people at 19 W. Mohawk Street

Afghan Idol—After nine years of success in the United States, the producers of American Idol have branched out with Afghan Idol. The series opens with 21 hopefuls, including Abdul Khaliq Aziz, Beltoon, Daud Noori ("Noori Dog"), Deepika Thathaal, Fiza Fayaz, Hafiz Karwandgar, Ibrahim Mohmand, Latif Nangarhari, Khan Qarabaghai, Mahjabeen Qazalbash, Mozhdah Jamalzadah, Noor Mohammad Kochai, Obaidullah Jan Kandarai, Peer Muhammad, Raees Khan, Sahibzada, Shafiq Mureed, Taj Khan, Valy Hedjasi, Wali Khan and Zia-ud-Din-Zia. The fun starts with the contestants belting out Afghan favorites such as "Kojahee" and "Jaan-e Maadar," while judges Randy Jackson, Jennifer Lopez and Steven Tyler try to figure out how to pronounce the contestants' names.

Who Wants to be Broke?—Spun off of the popular television show, 'Who Wants to be a Millionaire?', contestants verify their net worth to the producers prior to the start of the show. They then answer a series of increasingly difficult questions, betting their answers against their homes, cars, boats, vacation homes, children's college funds, life insurance policies and other valuable assets. When the contestant has been completely wiped out, they are sent home with a $100 gift certificate to Legal Zoom.

The Biggest Loser—Unlike the immensely popular reality show pitting personal trainer Jillian Michaels against obese people striving to lose weight, The Biggest Loser follows 20 slovenly, unemployed losers on welfare, food stamps and unemployment as they make their way through a typical day, bilking the system out of as much money as they can before they get caught by the police. The winner gets an all-expense paid vacation to the Los Angeles County court system that includes free uniforms, homemade shivs, 3 meals a day and free bus transportation between court dates.

Where the Sun Don't Shine

About the time I reached my fiftieth birthday, I experienced two inevitable milestones. The first was "The Letter" from AARP. The second was a reminder from my internist that it was time for my first sigmoidoscopy.

The AARP Letter magically appeared in my mailbox while I was in my late forties, inviting me to join the American Association of Retired People. It was the first time that I officially felt old. The week before, I was thinking about skydiving out of helicopters, running around with women half my age, racing formula one cars and skiing chest deep powder in Alaska. After getting The Letter, I became focused on reverse mortgages, adult diapers, support hose, tri-focal lenses, hearing aids, motorized scooters and burial sites.

Even though I'm now officially into middle age, I've put off having a sigmoidoscopy several times due to cost—or at least that was the best excuse I could come up with at the time. But, with health insurance companies now offering it as part of their preventative healthcare packages, my excuses were rapidly running out.

For the younger, uninitiated reader, a sigmoidoscopy is what healthcare professionals call a "routine" test—routine, if you consider shoving a tube, the length of a baseball bat into a place where the sun don't shine. The same reason why you never want to drop your soap in the shower at Sing Sing.

At the end of the tube is a camera that projects images of the real you onto a wide screen TV for a room full of giggling nursing students. There's also a long opening that runs down the length of the instrument where the gastroenterologist can insert a wire and "snip off" (his words, not mine) a little piece of the inside of your colon, should he discover something unusual. The official term is taking a biopsy. The unofficial term is shredding your bowels.

Still undaunted and ready to move ahead, my doctor explained to me how I'd need to prepare for the procedure. If the thought of having a vacuum cleaner hose pushed up your ying yang doesn't turn you off, then preparing your bowels for the exam will. My doc recommended that I stop by the pharmacy and pick up a HalfLytely Bowel Preparation kit. It comes in a large box, with all kinds of parts and instructions—lots of instructions. Ingesting a HalfLytely Bowel Preparation kit is the medical equivalent of having your bowels blown out by a fire hydrant. Even the fish sticks you ate in the sixth grade will somehow find their way out of your Adolf. They want your insides to be *clean*.

The Pharmacist ran through all of the standard HalfLytely precautions with me: don't wander too far from the bathroom, have only clear liquids the night before, don't wander too far from the bathroom, continue to take your regular medications, don't wander too far from the bathroom, drink plenty of water and don't wander too far from the bathroom. I somehow got the impression that I shouldn't wander too far from the bathroom.

The nurse told me that prior to the sigmoidoscopy, I'd need to arrive at the hospital early enough to fill out the usual medical history questionnaire: Do I now have or have I ever had heart disease, high blood pressure, diabetes, Shrinking Penis Syndrome, Mud Wrestlers Rash, Grocer's Itch, Uncombable Hair Syndrome, Mary Hart Epilepsy, Bowen's Disease, Fish Odor Syndrome, Carrot Addiction, Alien Hand Syndrome, Hula-hoop Intestine, Harlequin Ichthyosis, Nipple-Areolar Complex, Cutlery Craving, Foreign Accent Syndrome or Blue Skin Disorder? Sadly, I had to answer no to all of the above.

On the morning of the procedure, I was told to strip down and slip into a hospital gown—with the opening up the back. I had other things on my mind, so I had no problem with treating my fellow patients to a free view of my hairy derriere. After the nurse took my vital signs, she inserted an IV line and pushed in some sort of magic potion that made me feel like

I'd just polished off a 12-pack—in 3 minutes. The whole point of the sedative is to make you feel comfortable during the procedure and help you forget that you're about to be voluntarily violated.

After wheeling me into the operating room, the doctor asked me to roll onto my right side with my knees curled into the fetal position—the same position flight attendants instruct you take just before a fatal plane crash. While I was getting comfortable, I peeked over my shoulder and caught doc grinning from ear to ear as he greased up the dipstick. "Mr. Smith," he said. "When I insert the instrument, you may feel some mild discomfort. Just breathe normally and try to relax." Judging from the shredded Naugahyde on the operating table, the previous patients hadn't mastered this part. "You may want to hum one of your favorite songs to take your mind off of things," said the doctor. So, I chose two: "Tonight I want to Cry" by Keith Urban and "Deeper into You" by TrustCompany.

A minute later, I heard the air compressor start chugging away and contrary to his instructions, I clenched every muscle in my body (including my anal sphincter). The good doctor twisted and contorting his body as he guided the sigmoidoscope through the nooks and crannies of my digestive tract, yelling, "Whoa," "Whoo-hoo" and "Got you, ya bastard!" Was there an X-box in the OR?

The things no one prepared me for were the post-operative effects of someone inflating my lower intestinal tract like a truck tire. Within seconds after standing up, I cut loose with a toot that would have made the New York Philharmonic Orchestra green with envy. This was followed by the obligatory sprint for the restroom and more contributions from the wind section.

Thankfully, the results of the test came back negative for polyps and other irregularities, so I'm off the hook for another 5 years—just about long enough to recover my dignity.

A Hairdresser's Lament

In 1972, after two seasons as a ski lift operator at Mt. Snowsalot, I finally succumbed to my parents' complaints, "Why aren't you using that college education we paid for?" I explained to them that it was almost impossible to grab the first wrung of the corporate ladder with an Associate of Arts degree in Acne Rehabilitation. Nonetheless, I went on a mission to discover some purpose for my life

One of my earliest dreams had been to work for a ski resort. While my visions had me teaching skiing to voluptuous soap opera actresses, the best job I could find was a lift attendant—holding ski lift chairs steady, while guests plop their butts down as they're whisked away uphill. It's a pretty boring job. Unless someone dangles off of a fast moving chair from their underwear or gets pushed into the mud, there's not a lot to it. It didn't take long to realize that this was not the career I was looking for.

While I was parking butts on pads, I met a male hairdresser who seemed to have everything I wanted: lots of women, nice clothes, a new Porsche, lots of women, wads of cash, thick hair on his chest, gleaming teeth, lots of women, socks with no holes and an 8-track player in his car with the entire library of Three Dog Night. But, what really impressed me was that he could afford to live in a place without 18 roommates and eat something other than Top Ramen and peanut butter every night for dinner.

So, at the end of the ski season, I moved into a studio apartment with a dozen close friends and enrolled in The Hair Academy of Beverly Hills. I didn't do much research to see if it was a good school—I figured if it was in Beverly Hills, Tina Turner, Farrah Fawcett, Barbra Streisand, Diana Ross and Julie Christi were bound to walk through the doors. As it turned out, our school was located just on the fringe of Beverly Hills, in the seediest part of West Hollywood. I was heart-broken to learn that millionaire actresses don't get their hair done in beauty schools by people with three weeks of experience.

The first thing that surprised me about beauty school was how much there was to learn. Ms. Tulip was our primary instructor and had over 67 years of experience in the trenches—doing the hair of soldiers at Normandy on D-day. She would be leading us through 50 hours of general theory that included chemistry, sterilization techniques, infectious diseases and an introduction to skin and nail care. As it turned out, these were important things to know when they brought in the homeless women from the Los Angeles Rescue Mission for their monthly shearing. Most of the women hadn't had a shampoo since 1959, so we got a lot of practice de-lousing and ridding them of seborrhea, ringworm, psoriasis, lichen planus, lupus erthematosus, alopecia areata, acne and contact dermatitis—all of the things you'd expect to run into at an expensive Beverly Hills salon.

Twenty hours were required to learn "cold waving" or giving permanent waves. I don't know why they call it cold waving. With the number of screams you heard from the back shampoo bowls, you knew that when that perm solution singed their scalp, it felt anything but cool.

Getting a permanent wave from a beauty school student takes a lot of guts and not much money or sense. What you tended to end up with was something between the cute little hairdo Darla wore in "The Little Rascals," and the business end of a 40-year-old wart hog. I learned several important concepts during my permanent wave training—like not leaving the solution on too little or too long.

My first failure happened when I rinsed the perm solution out before it had completed its chemical process. So, Mrs. Belvedere left the school with hair sticking out at 45 degree angles all over her scalp. I compensated on the next client by leaving the solution on twice as long—resulting in my first "kick perm." A kick perm is one where the hair is wrapped around the rods so tightly that the rubber bands dissolve the hair right from the scalp. As each rod fell off onto the floor, my instructor Ms. Tulip taught me how to kick the rods underneath the sink before anyone had time to notice. Hence, the term, "kick perm."

The next challenge came in the form of 50 hours of hair coloring. As every elementary school student knows, all color starts out as some combination of three primary colors: red, green or blue. As a beginning cosmetology student, I found it was possible to expand these to include "moss-covered rock," "four month old pumpkin rinds" and "vomited fettuccini." To make it easy on me, Ms. Tulip started me out on blind women with almost no hair. It's hard to stray too far from the center line when the client can't see your results and an instructor with over 60 years of experience is hovering over you—nonetheless I managed to take hair where it had never gone before.

The results that left my booth after 9 months of hair coloring represented every imaginable (and unimaginable) color of the rainbow—none of which looked good on hair. "After a few shampoos, the brassiness will tone down a bit," became my standard comment as they ran out the front door covering their head with a Target bag. What the heck! It's not like I ever expected to see them again. Fortunately, the one thing you don't learn in beauty school is how to build repeat business, so it's off to the break room for another joint!

After weeks of annihilating my clients' hair, I was eager to spend 20 hours learning hair and scalp treatments. This was an opportunity to repair the damage I'd done to Mrs. Mordechai by applying soothing creams, lotions and salves to the burns I inflicted on her scalp. If she was lucky and her hair ever grew back, I'd give her a lecture on the importance of taking better care of her hair. As a horny guy in my 20s, I also found it to be a perfect opportunity to hit on the younger women. When they were laid back in a shampoo bowl with my fingers running through their hair, they'd agree to almost anything.

Following scalp treatments, came 20 hours of shampooing practice. Even though I had been washing my dog Scamper for years, I still had a few things to learn—like how to give a "proper" shampoo, how to position your client in the chair so you got the best view down her blouse, how to identify the shampoos they sell at Costco for 99-cents and the identical ones you'd get fleeced for at a high priced salon.

Shampooing is a great opportunity to wash away those nasty scabs and head lice while learning where all your client's moles are located. I learned how important water temperature was and came up with "Smith's Law." Smith's Law states that, "There is a direct relationship between how hot the water is and how far you can make your client jump out of their seat." It also works in reverse with ice cold water. I also realized the importance of a good aim. Nothing detracts from a nice hairstyle more than watching your client leave the salon with the back of her dress drenched down to her butt crack.

Then, came the fun part: 30 hours of hair cutting. Like hair coloring, I found it amazing how much destruction I could render in such a short period of time with little or no training. I also learned that if you sheared their hair too short, it was no big deal—by the time it grew back, I'd be long gone.

To get me started on the right foot, Ms. Tulip gave me women with little or no hair. Inevitably, they would bring in photos of themselves as a young girl in the 1930s, coiffed with finger waves and ask if I could duplicate it. Sure. No problem. We have a complete selection of wigs behind the cash register.

After a fun week of cutting hair, I faced the sobering task of 75 hours of giving facial treatments. Facials never held much interest for me. The thought of smearing $50 worth of goop around a woman's face made even less sense to me than smearing $50 worth of goop through their hair. But, I did find that it was another great way to hit on women, as they melted beneath my hovering fingers for an hour. I didn't learn much about skin care, but I maintained a pretty good batting average for home runs. Match.com has nothing on giving a woman an hour facial with Enya playing in the background.

The next part of my cosmetology training involved 35 hours of manicuring and pedicuring. I had been clipping my cat's toenails for years, so how hard could it be? Then Ms. Tulip brought me back to Earth by introducing terms like cuticles, nail beds and specialized equipment like cuticle clippers, emery boards, buffers, scissors, orange sticks, rubber thimbles, cuticle removers, massage lotions, base coats, nail polish, top coats, stick on jewels, polish remover, hand cream, sanitizing sprays, cotton balls and hand towels. I also learned that professional cosmetologists don't rip off their client's cuticles with their front teeth.

After weeks of practicing manicuring and pedicuring, I developed my own unique technique for applying nail polish. Instead of meticulously brushing polish on the nails, I found it was easier just to dip the client's entire finger into the top of the bottle and wipe away the excess with a towel. The technique worked well until it came to thumbs and toes—then I'd just pour it on.

With 37 weeks of intense instruction under my belt, I could almost see light at the end of the tunnel. There was only one skill yet to be learned: waxing. Waxing is a method of "permanently" removing hair from an area of the body using hot bees wax, covered in gauze. It's popular for men and women on eyebrows, the upper lip, face, legs, arms, under arms, the back, abdomen, feet and unmentionable areas using Brazilian hot waxing. None of the female students would let me practice that on them, so I had to wait until I got home to try it on Scamper.

The benefits of waxing mean that your client can more or less forget shaving an area for weeks at a time. While most salons describe waxing as a mildly uncomfortable experience, those who have actually had it done compare it with being scalped at Little Big Horn. And then, of course, there are the drawbacks. While in school, I had to practice on my locker mate, Phil. We determined that waxing his entire back would give me all the credits I needed for the entire semester and leave his back as smooth as a baby's bottom. After a few of us managed to scrape Phil off of the ceiling, I reminded him that even though his skin was as smooth and silky today, three days from now, his back was likely to be engulfed in ingrown hairs, red bumps, blackheads, minor bleeding and a blood infection. It's best to explain these things after your client's already had the procedure done.

Graduation day from The Hair Academy of Beverly Hills came and went without fanfare. With over 100 other students, Ms. Tulip was too busy repairing kick perms and breaking up the cat fights in the women's locker room to give me anything more than a handshake and a shove out the door. But she did manage to help me land my first job at "Hair Today—Gone Tomorrow." The rest is history.

The Ever-Changing Dating Game

When Adam and Eve ventured out on their first date, romance was considerably easier than it is today. There weren't other men and women to compete against, they didn't have to be concerned with what clothes to wear and Lucifer took care of the dinner arrangements.

Since that infamous first date, the process of finding "the one" has endured countless twists, turns and dead ends. Gold miners in the 1860s quickly learned that they could bypass the entire dating scene by ordering a bride through the mail. They not only got a lady who would put up with their poor hygiene but they could also buy someone who was willing to accommodate gaps in their manners larger than the spaces between their teeth. In the 1920s, "modern" dating took the form of socializing in group settings like church gatherings, community dances and hay rides. Relationships typically began with a suitor paying a visit to the young woman's home where she received him in the family parlor—chaperoned by her mother, father, grandmother, grandfather, pastor, 6 aunts and uncles, 8 brothers and sisters 12 dogs and 15 cats. The relationship culminated by the exchange of a dowry: usually a cow, a pig, $25 and a dozen eggs.

During World War II, dapper young American soldiers wooed innocent European ladies in crisp military uniforms and shoes so shiny they reflected the Lucky Strikes dangling from their lips. After the war (and a brief courtship), the soldiers returned to the U.S. with their new wives in tow. The brides quickly learned dozens of quaint American customs like pumping out kids one after the other, scrubbing the kitchen floor, washing loads of dirty laundry, picking up dog shit from the back yard and heating up TV dinners.

In my parents' generation, men and women showed respect for each other by navigating through a complicated set of dating conventions that began with formal introductions between the elders of two families. It progressed to love letters delivered by snail mail, weekly telephone calls, followed by a year of chaperoned dates. Today, randy men and women can fast forward through awkward first dates by flirting on dozens of online dating sites like Match.com, eHarmony, Pentyoffish.com, Chemistry.com and Craigslist. From the comfort of their stained sweatpants, overweight, unemployed losers with inferiority complexes can pretend to be virile, Harvard-educated orthopedic surgeons without the fear of ever having to actually meet anyone in person.

Singles on the prowl also need to master technologies that have infiltrated the modern dating scene—like text and instant messaging. Text messaging has replaced writing intimate letters in longhand and allows two people to trade innuendos as fast as their pudgy fingers can race across a keyboard the size of a postage stamp. But, to play the game you need to learn a new language: text message abbreviations. Ten years ago a girl might have sent the following letter to her love interest, accompanied by a single, red rose:

Hi Jeff,

How are you? What's been filling your days? I loved hearing from you and I think you have a wonderful sense of humor. Your last letters tickled me and made me laugh. As you know, I'm looking for that special someone. Could you be the one? How about finally meeting face to face? Let's meet in real life to talk about a beginning a long-term relationship, OK? I'll be at Starbucks at 4:00 PM. I'll be the one with the short mini-skirt and no underwear. Well, that's it for now, so I'll talk to you later. Please send me a note if you can make it. Bye bye for now. Beatrice.

Today, people skip the hand-written note and flowers and dash off a quick text message while stuck in traffic:

HJ . . . Hig? Wayd? I loved hearing from u and think u have a gsoh. Your last 2 tm had me rotflmao. Ayk, I'm looking for that special some1. Could u be the 1? How about meeting f2f? Lmirl to talk about a ltr, ok? I'll be at *bucks at 4. I'll be the 1 w/ the smsnuw. Well, tafn so I'll ttul. Smaim if you can make it. Bb4n. B.

If all of your best efforts end in disaster, there's no reason to sulk. There are plenty of contemporary ways to handle rejection. Gone are the days of enduring that "Dear John" letter during final examinations. Instead, you can publicly humiliate your ex on the Internet. If you own a digital camera (and who doesn't?), you can post embarrassing photos of psycho-bitch caught on the toilet or wrapped in the arms of Raul, the tennis pro at exgirlfriendrevenge.net, revengesex.net or myexisabitch.com. There's even a handy self-help section on sweetrevengenow.com that will not only provide you with tips on how to get back at your cheating lover (subscribe them to 300 magazines or have 75 large pizzas delivered to their office) but also offers the newly jilted a complete line of revenge products like simulated doggie poo or a hand-crafted voo doo doll, complete with pins.

Customs, Laws and Faux Pas

Have you ever wondered why when an infant burps after their morning bottle we all think it's so cute? Yet, forty years later, the same guy belching after his eighteenth tallboy is absolutely disgusting? Why does a case of unbridled hiccups crack up everyone at the dinner table, but a well-placed air biscuit can clear the room? Like most other societies, American customs have resulted from generations of rules, laws, faux pas and in some cases, no reason at all.

Many of our customs date far back before you were even a twinkle in your mother's eye. These were times of unsophisticated knowledge and religious beliefs. Mores and values were often steeped in superstition and fear. For instance, people saying "God bless you" after a sneeze, is a byproduct of the epidemics that devastated entire countries during the Middle Ages. Sneezing was usually the first sign that the victim was coming down with the bubonic plague. Friends and family would mutter, "God bless you," just before sprinting for the safety of the nearest dungeon. I'm happy to say that some of these customs still exist today.

Each civilization had their own unique customs. In ancient Japan, public contests were held in small towns to see who could "break wind" the loudest and longest. Winners were awarded prizes and great acclaim, of course, yards away from the nearest open flame. In some parts of Java, couples had sex in the fields to promote crop growth (sometimes called "plowing the back 40"). And in other cultures, the wedding cake was originally thrown at the bride and groom, instead of eaten by them.

At one time in India, a fiancé was required to deflower his future bride post-mortem if she died before the wedding. The girl could not be cremated until this ritual was carried out in front of the village priest. The

Ankole people of Uganda took their bedroom responsibilities seriously. One custom required that the aunt of the groom teach the prospective bride everything she knew about pleasing a man—both in and out of the bedroom. In the case of slow learners, aunts would often share the bed with the couple on their wedding night—just to make sure the bride got everything right. On the flip side, the best gift that the father of the groom could give his son was assistance by sleeping with the bride before the wedding night.

The Tidong from northern Borneo have an uncomfortable wedding custom that dictates that neither the bride nor the groom can use the bathroom for the three days leading up to the wedding ceremony—no urinating, defecating or bathing. It's thought that the practice leads to a long, happy and fertile marriage—and helps to conserve on toilet paper.

Blessing the new couple takes a number of forms, depending on where you're married. In Tudor times, guests would throw their shoes at the bride and groom as they fled their wedding celebration. Anyone hit by these flying projectiles inherited good luck. During Anglo Saxon times, the groom would establish his authority over the household by striking the bride with a shoe. And, in Scotland, guests revel in "Blackening the Bride," an old tradition of dousing the bride in a stinky mixture of eggs, flour, sauces and feathers, then parading her around town as the wedding guests beat on bowls and drums.

In addition to unusual wedding customs, many parts of the world have enjoyed practices that would undoubtedly be difficult to accept in America. In certain parts of Greece, people would spit three times in the face of anyone deserving a compliment. The purpose of spitting was to ward off evil spirits and bad luck.

And, in Turkey during the 16th and 17th centuries, anyone caught drinking coffee was put to death. It's a good thing Starbucks waited a few hundred years before hiring their first Barista.

Now, before you judge other countries harshly, think about some of the laws that used to (or still do) exist in the United States:

- Having sexual relations with a porcupine is illegal in Florida.
- Every citizen of Kentucky is required to take at least one bath a year.
- It's illegal to hunt camels in the state of Arizona.
- In Arkansas, a man is free to beat his wife once a month.
- It is a misdemeanor in California to shoot any game from a moving vehicle unless the target is a whale.
- Cat owners of Sterling, Colorado must insure that if their cat goes outside unattended, it is equipped with a tail light.
- Citizens of Devon, Connecticut are prohibited from walking backwards after sunset.
- Anyone getting married on a dare in Delaware has grounds for an annulment.
- It is against the law for Florida residents to dream about another man's wife or cow.
- You cannot tie your giraffe to a telephone pole in Georgia.
- Twins in Hawaii cannot work for the same company.
- In Idaho, boxes of candy given as romantic gifts must weight at least 50 lbs.
- Hat pins, like switchblade knives, are considered illegal, concealed weapons in Chicago.
- Gary, Indiana theaters prohibit anyone from attending within four hours of eating onion or garlic.
- Iowa laws prohibit any man with a moustache from kissing a woman in public.
- Concealed bean snappers are illegal in Wichita, Kansas.
- In Kentucky, it's illegal for women to marry the same man four times.
- Louisiana laws prohibit anyone from gargling in public or wearing an alligator costume.
- Portland, Maine men may not tickle women under their chins with a feather duster.
- In Maryland, it's illegal to mistreat oysters (except to eat them).
- Boston churchgoers risk arrest if they eat peanuts in church.
- Detroit residents may not make love in their car, unless it's parked on their property.
- In International Falls, Minnesota, owners of dogs can be fined for allowing their pets to chase cats up telegraph poles.

- Oxford, Mississippi law forbids anyone from spitting on the sidewalks.
- In Excelsior Springs, Missouri, it is illegal to make a squirrel worry.
- A woman's clothes must weigh more than 3 lbs 2 oz before she can legally dance on a Helena, Montana saloon table.
- Lehigh, Nebraska law prohibits anyone from selling donut holes.
- In Las Vegas, Nevada, it is prohibited to pawn your dentures.
- Residents of New Hampshire may not dye their margarine pink.
- Trenton, New Jersey law makes it illegal to throw bad pickles into the street.
- In Carrizozo, New Mexico, it is illegal for women to appear unshaven in public.
- A New York City law allows both men and women to ride the subway topless.
- Asheville, North Carolina residents are prohibited from sneezing within city limits.
- Residents of North Dakota are prohibited from falling asleep with their shoes on.
- Ohio law prohibits anyone from fishing for whales on Sundays.
- Cars must be tethered outside of Oklahoma buildings.
- Portland, Oregon residents are prohibited from whistling underwater.
- In Philadelphia, Pennsylvania, people are banned from putting pretzels in bags.
- In Rhode Island, it's illegal to throw pickle juice while riding on a trolley.
- South Carolina residents must be 18 years of age to play pinball.
- South Dakota law prohibits anyone from falling asleep in a cheese factory.
- Tennessee fishermen are prohibited from lassoing fish.
- In many parts of Texas, it is illegal to sell one's eye.
- Birds have the right of way on Utah highways.
- Vermont women must get written permission from their husbands before wearing false teeth.
- Unmarried Virginia residents having sex, risk arrest under a class 4 misdemeanor.

- Lynden, Washington residents are prohibited from dancing and drinking in the same establishment.
- Snoozing on a train is illegal in West Virginia.
- Women in St. Croix Wisconsin may not wear red clothing in public.
- It is illegal to tickle women in Wyoming.

Many of these laws remain on the books to this day. Why? Who knows? But just as soon as they decide to remove the law, someone in Arizona is going to wing a camel while driving out of Phoenix on Interstate 10.

Hypochondriacs Make Me Sick

I got up this morning with a sore throat—again. Most people with a sore throat don't think anything about it. They take two aspirins and get ready for work. But, I'm different. Instead of interpreting my discomfort for what it really is—something minor that will be over in a few days—my mind starts racing, imagining the worst case scenario. What happens if it's something serious like *throat cancer*? Or paraneoplastic pemphigus, microcephaly, Fibrodysplasia ossificans progressive or Field's disease? I don't even know what those are, but the Discovery Channel said they were serious.

If it does turn out to be one of those hard to pronounce diseases, I'll have to quit work, break up with my girlfriend, sell my car, cancel all my subscriptions to Better Home and Gardens, National Geographic, Family Circle, People Magazine, Prevention, Oprah Magazine, Martha Steward Living and the TV Guide. And, since time is rapidly running out, I might as well give away all of my belongings—except the things I'll need for my final days, like my hospital gowns, slippers and my IV pole.

As it always turns out, there's never anything wrong with me. But some people aren't so lucky. When you find yourself fearing the worst, think about the poor people with these diseases and what they have to look forward to each day:

Capgras Syndrome

Capgras Syndrome was first discovered by Dr. Joseph Capgras in 1923 when one of his patients complained that doubles, or other people, had taken the place of her and her husband. The syndrome often makes victims suspicious of reflections in the mirror—including their own. They'll see their reflections in shiny surfaces and wonder who the stranger is that's peering back at them. As part of a larger family of diseases like schizophrenia, epilepsy or malformed temporal lobes of the brain, Capgras Syndrome patients often have trouble making connections with people, places and things—even if they've been in their lives for years. Capgras Syndrome patients often convince themselves that someone has broken into their home and replaced familiar objects like pets or shoes with imposters.

Foreign Accent Syndrome

One of the most intriguing psychological diseases on record is one that allows you to acquire a foreign language—overnight. The first patient with Foreign Accent Syndrome was a Norwegian woman diagnosed in 1941, who sustained a shrapnel injury during the Second World War. Even though she had never been out of Norway, she woke up one morning speaking perfect German—including the accent. Unfairly, she was shunned by her family and friends. Eventually, she conquered a neighboring village.

Linda Walker was a 60 year old woman from Newcastle, UK who was also stricken with Foreign Accent Syndrome during a stroke. Following successful recovery, Linda would randomly lapse from her normal, Geordie accent into Jamaican, French Canadian, Slovak or Italian.

In 2008, Cindy Romberg of Port Angeles, Washington was featured on the Discovery Health Channel after she was stricken with Foreign Accent Disease following a neck adjustment from her chiropractor. She began speaking with a Russian accent, even making the predictable grammatical mistakes of a Russian attempting to speak English.

Alien Hand Syndrome

If ever there was a disease that a horny high school boy would crave, it would be Alien Hand Syndrome. Also known as Dr. Strangelove Syndrome, victims of Alien Hand Syndrome find that one of their hands operates completely and independently from the rest of their body—sometimes against their will. Caused by damage to the parietal or occipital lobe of the brain, AHS sufferers complain of having rogue hands—hands that will often undo buttons and remove clothing, as if by their own volition. One patient reported a bizarre incident where her right hand put a cigarette into her mouth. Before she could light it, her left hand yanked the cigarette out and crushed it in an ashtray.

Pica

It's almost a right of passage for small children to eat an occasional handful of dirt. For normal kids, it's just a phase. But for those stricken with Pica, eating dirt and other non-food items becomes a dangerous part of their lives. It is often associated with children younger than 24 months, epileptics and some pregnant women.

People who suffer with Pica not only eat dirt, but are also attracted to a variety of non-food items like cigarette butts, soap, paper, buttons, glue, sand, hair, paint chips, plaster and even feces—all varieties. Undoubtedly, the most documented case of Pica involved a man with Cutlery Craving. The 47-year-old Englishman underwent more than 30 operations to remove 8 dinner forks and a mop head from his stomach.

One form of Pica called Geophagia is regularly practiced by cultures that eat substances such as dirt and clay to control diarrhea, morning sickness, relieve nausea and to remove toxins from their bodies.

Fish Odor Syndrome

Everyone's entitled to episodes of bad breath, body odor or flatulence. But, how would you like to go through your entire life smelling of putrid fish? A rare, but documented medical disorder called Fish Odor Syndrome (also called trimethylaminuria or TMAU) results from an enzyme called trimethylamine passing through your sweat, urine or breath, that results in a strong fishy odor. Research indicates that Fish Odor Syndrome is more prevalent in women than men and is often linked to the female sex hormones estrogen or progesterone.

There is no cure for Fish Odor Syndrome, but there are some things sufferers can do to control the disease. By avoiding legumes, eggs and other foods that contain sulfur, nitrogen and choline, patients can minimize its unsavory symptoms. And, of course, showering regularly never hurts.

Uncombable Hair Syndrome

If you get upset over an infrequent bad hair day, consider yourself lucky. Think about the unfortunate people who are afflicted with Uncombable Hair Syndrome. There have been fewer than 60 diagnosed cases of Uncombable Hair Syndrome between 1973 and 1998. It typically affects young boys and girls before puberty and is considered an inherited disease, being passed from one generation to the next. The trouble begins when the hair follicle produces triangular (instead of round) hair shafts, with longitudinal grooves. The hair contains very little pigment and is very dry and brittle. Uncombable hair rarely lies down. Instead it grows at right angles from the scalp.

What should you do if you've been stricken with Uncombable Hair Syndrome? The first thing is cancel your appointment with your hairdresser. Then, find a trichologist or a dermatologist who is familiar with the disease. People suffering from UHS may also experience alopecia, baldness and find that their hair breaks off before it has time to grow. The good news is that some cases recover spontaneously several years after it first appears.

Considering how bad things could really be with my smell, accent, diet and hair, I decided to take a couple of aspirin, gargle some Listerine, wrap a thick, wool muffler around my neck and trudge off to work. After all, things could be worse.

The Breast of Times

I'm a healthy, red-blooded man, so it's natural that I think a lot about women's breasts. You know: babaloos, bazookas, bijongas, boulders, chi-chis and Danny Devitos. Flapdoodles, headlamps, hooters, jugs, Lewinskis, chumbawumbas and milk bombs. Nose warmers, shirt puppies, tatas, dinglebobbers and torpedoes. Whatever you choose to call them, they're the most alluring part of a woman's body—the part that's always on my mind. And, apparently, I'm not alone.

Men and women have been thinking about boobsters for about as long as they've been adorning women's chests. Although no one was there to record it, I'm sure that after his first fateful bite of the apple, Adam said to Eve, "Hey, Eve. Nice rack you've got there!" Rock carvings and statues featuring women's cantaloupes have been recorded as far back as 15,000 BC. Even the male Egyptian river god Hapy was depicted with cupcakes. This explains the ancient Egyptian saying, "Have a Hapy day!"

Throughout history, a woman's dumplings were traditionally displayed au naturel, until the Greeks began covering women's bodies both in their art and in the flesh. Of course, there were exceptions, like Aprodite, the Goddess of Love, who freely displayed her dairy pillows—albeit in a posture that portrayed shyness and modesty. It took thousands of years and American ingenuity before a woman's funbags were put on display again in topless bars, strip clubs, Las Vegas extravaganzas, on television and in the movies.

Whether they're small, medium or large, women are constantly on the lookout for ways to enhance the appearance of their gazongas. And over time, they've taken some drastic measures to ensure that they look their best.

Long before breast implants became available to the general public, women clambered for ways to make their goombas look bigger. Their cries for help were answered in the early 1970s by the Foot Operated Breast Enlarger. Women pining for bigger hood ornaments spent $9.95 for something that was nothing more than a foot-operated vacuum pump and a series of cups that promised, "larger, firmer and more shapely breasts in only 8 weeks." Over four million women were duped into purchasing the device that produced little more than bruising—even if they opted for the one ounce bottle of "Cleavage 6 Breast Enhancement" potion.

During the 1960s, two ingenious entrepreneurs named Jack and Eileen Feather began marketing their "Mark Eden Bust Developer" through the Mark Eden Company that **" . . . guaranteed to add three inches to your bustline."** The device was nothing more than two clamshell-shaped pieces of plastic, separated by a spring. Women wanting bigger knockers pressed the two clamshells together with their arms and patiently waited for the results. At $9.95, the Mark Eden Bust Developer was a pretty good deal. It just didn't work.

One of the issues with the Mark Eden Bust Developer was the lack of scientific research backing up its claims. Mr. Feather tested it on his wife (who was already endowed well enough not to need it) and a few clients at his figure salons. With his imagination in overdrive, and noticing some "subtle transformation in his clients," the Mark Eden Bust Developer was ready to take on the world.

To help market his Bust Developer, Mr. Feather hired June Wilkinson, a famous actress of the day. After paying her $1,000 and 25 cents for every unit sold, Ms. Wilkinson declared to the world, "There is an incomparable difference in the entire feminine line, shape, and grace of my whole figure. My very presence has taken on a new and subtle glow of womanliness, of sex-appeal, and yes, of glamour that is undeniable and unmistakable."

The Bust Developers sold well, until one by one, women began returning them. Mainly because they weren't seeing results. Refunding the money wasn't a problem until the U.S. Postal Service received dozens of consumer complaints. After selling over 18,000 Bust Developers, the U.S.

Government eventually shut down the Mark Eden operation and issued an order of fraud.

During the court hearings, dozens of scientific experts for each side paraded to and from the witness stand, challenging Mr. Eden's "scientific breakthrough" in breast enhancement. It turned out that the only things the Breast Enhancer was capable of enlarging was the muscles in a woman's back. Not many of Mr. Eden's customers were interested in having more muscular backs. And, so went the demise of the Mark Eden Bust Developer.

More recently, there have been a new crop of products claiming to enhance the appearance of a woman's honkers. Telebrands is currently selling the Bare Lifts Instant Breast Lift on TV. The Lifts are pairs of sticky tape that you press onto your boulders, just above the nipple. Then, you pull the tape up and stick it on your chest. While it doesn't claim to actually change the make-up of a woman's chi-chis, it will instantly " . . . lift the breasts, ensuring a naturally perky look in any outfit. You can lift each breast and realign your nipple to a higher position, even if you are larger than a D cup." The only problem is, the kit doesn't come with a carpenter's level, so it's very easy to position one puppy higher than the other.

On the more conservative side, there are dozens of breast enlargement pills, lotions and creams. There's even a handy website, www.breastenhancementpills.org, that will help you ferret out the differences between Breast Success, Bust Fuel, Confident Curves, Grobust, Naturmam, Total Curve, Revitabust and Voluptas.

For women who are ready to make a serious commitment to having bigger, more shapely sweater puppies, surgical breast augmentation is the answer. There are skilled surgeons in every corner of the world who will be happy to do the job for as little as $5,000-$15,000, letting you choose between silicon and saline solution implants.

When it comes to a women's figure, nothing is more important than her tatas. And, thanks to American ingenuity, there are almost as many solutions as there are slang terms for them. Isn't America grand?

On Becoming A Famous Writer

Being an internationally acclaimed writer, I'm constantly stopped by people and asked, "How do you write?" "How do you come up with such great ideas?" or "What's your cholesterol level?"

One of the greatest challenges of being a professional writer is constantly coming up with new ideas for articles that other people find interesting enough to read. Writing about the Pope's visit, airline crashes, unemployment, foreign affairs and politics bore my readers, so I owe it to them to delve into more obscure topics. For instance, during the hype of the 2007 Tour de France (historically an all male event), I wrote an article about the first time officials let women compete for the maillot jaune. Naturally, significant changes had to be made—like re-routing the course through the best shopping districts, adding emergency acrylic nail repair stations to the course and requiring all female contestants to complete wind tunnel tests to insure that their breasts weren't giving them an unfair advantage over other contestants. You get the idea.

A lot of well know authors will tell you that it's important to have a good place to write—one that's comfortable and stimulates your imagination. I get a lot of my best ideas in the shower. So, I've moved my desk, telephone and laptop into my shower stall. When I hit a dry spell for ideas, I just take a shower. Over the years, long, hot showers have produced ideas for 17 Academy Award winning screenplays such as "The Grandfather," "Slumdog Destitutes," "Ben's-Hair," "Schindler's Grocery List," "The Ten Commencements" and "The Sound of Rap Music."

When a great idea comes to me, I have to seize the opportunity immediately. That's why I have a number of laptops in my home—one in every room. I also keep an iPad in my car, 4 iPhones, a pad of paper and a pencil. The interior of my house is covered with little sticky notes with ideas that go back to the early 1960s—I like to call them my works in progress. If an idea comes into my head, I immediately stop what I'm doing, go home and start writing. For instance, in 1993, I was reading a passage of my book, "Spooning in Afghanistan" during the Kennedy Center Honors. In the middle of a passage, the idea for another work, "The Leper Story," came to me, so I abruptly left the stage and went home to write. The result was my 4th Academy Award winning screenplay.

While the shower may be where I get my ideas, it's not where I prefer to write. I recently bought a used Honda Accord that has become a very productive, mobile writing studio. I've found when I get the itch to write, I can turn on the cruise control and steer with my bare feet while balancing my laptop in between my knees. When things are going well, I can transcribe a recent interview onto my laptop, take a conference call on my cell phone, text my girlfriend and eat lunch—all while speeding down the Pacific Coast Highway.

Unlike other writers, I don't write my works from beginning to end. Instead, I start at the middle. By the time the characters have matured and the plot has thickened in the middle of the work, they've already established the most important elements. It's easy then to write backwards to the beginning and forward to the end. I find that it keeps the plot fresh and better accommodates my bi-polar personality.

A well known problem, even outside of writing circles, is writer's block. I don't believe in it. However, I do believe in writer's constipation and diarrhea. Writer's block is a theoretical condition where the writer feels unable to write—there's a paucity of ideas that stop somewhere between the brain and the printed page. It's also another term for laziness. I should know. No one's lazier than me, and even I don't experience writer's block. I do, however, sympathize with writers who claim that they suffer from this dilemma. When writing comes slowly to me (and it rarely does) there are things I can do to get the juices flowing again.

I find ideas for articles everywhere. The first thing that I do after getting up at noon is peruse the newspapers headlines to see what's making news.

Any subject that's recently reached the public eye is ripe for a new story. For example, here are a couple of headlines that resulted in two of my five Pulitzer Prizes:

First man in space: A 50-year-old feat remembered. In the 1960s, getting to space was a big deal. These days, space shuttles run more frequently than Southwest Airlines flights—and their ceilings don't rip off in mid-flight. I wrote an article about how adult diapers helped to get astronaut John Glenn back in space after a 50-year hiatus. I peppered the piece with a few well-placed anecdotes from other astronauts living in the NASA retirement home about how they depended on duct tape to make their missions go smoothly.

Australia proposes tough cigarette packaging rules. The public has had it when it comes to pressuring tobacco companies to market their products in a more responsible way to children, emphysema patients, death row inmates, prostitutes, cancer victims and others hooked on cigarette smoking. I wrote a piece for the Washington Post about the recent round of Australian legislation that requires cigarette manufacturers to de-glamorize smoking by putting graphic illustrations of dead babies, black lungs and sickly children on the labels. I went on to discuss how the United States could jump on the bandwagon by sealing cigarettes in impregnable material that requires a special tool for opening. The tool would only be available for purchase at offices of the American Lung Association for $499.

Admittedly, one of the down sides of my extraordinary writing career has been fame, fortune and all of the responsibilities that go with them. Before I wrote my Golden Globe winning screenplay for "The Rings of Uranus," I enjoyed the simple pleasures of anonymity—sitting unnoticed in a holding cell, arguing with the Baristas at Starbucks, being able to piss on the side of a building and scattering my trash on the floor at Burger King. After I was nominated for the Nobel Prize in Drama, I had to learn how to live life on different terms.

One of the books I'd recommend to new writers learning how to deal with fame is Sadam Hussein's "Keep On Moving—How I Managed to Stay Alive for a Year in a Ditch." The book is loaded with tips like sleeping underneath a different house every night, ways to deal with your enemies and getting back at the press. There is an entire section devoted to concocting innovative disguises like burn victims, plane crash survivors and mobsters through creative make-up techniques. There's also a very useful chapter on how to deal with depression, bad moods, acting out on fantasies, crying over nothing, lack of concentration, stomach problems, paranoia and self-hatred—just some of the rewards of becoming a famous writer.

Golf Course Thugs

I love sports. And, considering there isn't an athletic gene in my entire family, I manage to do pretty well at anything I decide to try—except golf.

Looking back, I'm not really sure why I took up golf in the first place. It's the one sport that, the harder I tried, the worse I got. I was in high school at the time and started hanging around a tough bunch of thugs. Well, not really thugs as you know them. We weren't covered with tattoos, didn't wear smelly leather jackets, take drugs or hang around street corners fleecing old ladies of their social security checks. None of us had motorcycles, so there wasn't any point in planning a bank robbery with a high speed getaway. But we did terrorize golfers at our local pitch and putt.

One of the first things that drew me to golf was all of the cool stuff you needed in order to play the game. There were the clubs, the golf club bags with all of the zippers and handles, the spiked shoes, tees, balls (that came in a nice cellophane-wrapped box), gloves, clothes and hats. Then, there were all of the accessories: rangefinders, golf ball retrievers, knitted golf club head covers, golf towels, umbrellas, watches, carts, stands and training accessories.

I also liked golf because you could drink beer and smoke while playing the game—pretty tough to do with other sports like pole vaulting or running steeplechase. My parents were very supportive of my getting involved with golf. They thought it was great that I hung around the clubhouse and driving range everyday after school—at least until they discovered what I was really up to.

Tom, Ted and I were the Three Musketeers of golf. We started out by sharing one set of women's clubs between the three of us and headed for the driving range. For those of you who have never played golf, a driving range is a place where you stand side by side, next to your fellow golfers, humiliating yourself while trying to look cool. For a few bucks, you can buy a small basket of "range balls." These are balls that someone paid $50 for yesterday and have since been rescued from the bottom of a scummy pond, sand trap or extricated from a chain link fence. They're easily identifiable by their moss-green color, nicks and gouges from being run over by the lawn mowers.

Golf is all about looking cool and there are a lot of ways to accomplish this. First, cool golfers never run anywhere—they lumber. If someone threw burning napalm on them, a serious golfer would still lumber to the waiting ambulance. Staying up on the latest fashions is another great way to look cool. Because we hadn't as yet landed our first professional sponsor, we started out wearing blue jeans, tennis shoes and T-shirts, but quickly liberated our first golf knickers, plaid vests and beanies from the men's locker room. After all, if you don't know what you're doing, at least you can look like you do.

So, we lumbered out to the driving range in our new outfits, still missing golf spikes. Golf spikes are shoes with sharp nails protruding from the bottoms, so you want to make sure you don't wear them onto your mother's linoleum kitchen floor. I made that mistake—once. Since golf spikes are essentially really expensive shoes, our first pair came out of the lost and found. I found an empty bag of Scott's Turf Builder and stuffed it into the toes until I could afford a pair that fit right.

The idea behind the spikes is to help you maintain traction on the grass during your swing. In my case, I could have worn hip waders—nothing would have made much difference. But, while you're on the driving range, golf spikes make you look like you know what you're doing until the first time you trip over your own feet.

To look cool on the driving range, I discovered how to bend over at the waist, balancing over my right leg, with my hand on the end of the golf club as I "teed up" my ball. That's golf talk for balancing a small round object on the top of an even tinier, little wooden stick. To make it a little more exciting, we skipped the tees and took turns lying down, balancing the ball on our pursed lips. The guy with the best aim got to drive the rest of us to the Emergency Room.

One of the first things we learned about actually playing the game is the importance of etiquette. Not only are there hundreds of rules that pertain to course play, there are dozens of unclassified faux pas both on and off the course. This is where we began to run afoul with the golf course marshals. For us, all of those rules made the game stuffy and were meant to be broken. Take the first tee, for example.

During traditional play, the player teeing up for their shot is extended absolute silence until they've completed their stroke. We decided it would be more challenging and a lot more fun if we were allowed to jump up and down, wave our arms and yell, trying to break each other's concentration. Boom boxes, whoopee cushions, compressed air horns and igniting M-80s were all perfectly legal. Anything went as long as you didn't physically contact the player teeing off—yet.

Once we all successfully teed off, we began the "full contact" aspect of the game. While Tom was sauntering down the fairway trying to find his ball, Ted ran up from behind and cross-body blocked him behind his knees, sending his clubs flying across the fairway. While Ted's attention was tied up on Tom, I hurried over to his ball and ground it three inches into the turf like an old cigarette butt. After repositioning his dislocated knee, Tom brushed himself off and was able to continue limping along by tying his golf sweater around his knee, as a makeshift brace. But, Ted had problems locating his ball. After an hour had passed, he ceded and we made him go back to the first tee to start over.

While we were waiting for Ted, a thick layer of fog rolled onto the second fairway, making the green impossible to see. So, after pulling the short straw, Tom "volunteered" to stand out in the middle of the fairway, completely engulfed in fog. Since we couldn't begin to estimate where the green lie, we told him to keep singing "We Gotta Get Out of This Place" so we'd know in which direction to hit. We coined this "Fog Golf," and have only run into two other people dumb enough to play it.

The official golf rule book states, "Play the ball as it lies, play the course as you find it, and if you cannot do either, do what is fair." We instituted a "no maximum number of strokes" rule that usually led to some pretty high scoring games. On one occasion, Ted drove the ball over a chain link fence, onto a neighbor's roof. By the time he returned his ball into play, he was already up 45 strokes—and it was only the third hole.

It had rained on the course the night before, so the fairways were lined with 3-foot deep puddles that added to the challenge of the sand traps. I managed to lob my ball into the center of one of these puddles and had to take off my shoes, socks and pants before wading into the water. If you've ever tried to hit a golf ball that is resting at the bottom of a three foot puddle, you're in for a treat. My first 14 or 15 strokes looked like Moses parting the Red Sea—6 foot walls of water arched toward the sky, while my ball lay contently on the bottom of the ditch. After 30 minutes, I had driven so much water out of the trench that I was finally able to advance my ball several inches toward the green.

Over the next few months, we added running and tackling our opponents in between holes as a way to add more sport to the game. As soon as the last of the party teed off, we were off and running. Tackling, body blocking, tripping and pushing your opponents were all legal play. At the end of the round, we'd tally up not only the number of strokes, but also deducted points for the least amount of time it took to get from the first tee to the final putt.

By the time we got back to the clubhouse, it was well after dark, so luckily none of the people on the driving range saw the blood, Tom's bandaged leg or my sopping wet clothes. After we settled up at with clubhouse for the damage to the trees and broken windows, we headed for home, noticing that there were three police cars in the parking lot. Apparently, someone had stolen some expensive golf outfits from the men's locker room.

The Great Sperm Audition

During tough economic times, difficult problems require creative solutions. It's important to honestly take stock of your current skills and decide what you have to offer society that's easily convertible into a livable wage. That's why I was so intrigued when I ran across an article in the Washington Post, with the following headlines:

"Fertility Clinics are Facing a 'National Crisis' Because of a Shortage of Sperm Donors"

While I'd like to admit that my heart went out to all of the unfortunate couples who couldn't conceive children on their own, in truth, it was my interest in self-centered preservation that was piqued. I could literally be sitting on a goldmine of untapped resources. Well, maybe not sitting on it, but very close by.

Donating sperm sounded perfect for me. After all, the hours are flexible, it's something that I already do well, one hand wouldn't have to know what the other is doing and I wouldn't be against putting in overtime—for the good of those poor unfortunate couples. As far as I could tell, the only drawback would be admitting to people that my life revolved entirely around masturbation. Nevertheless, I decided to look into it.

Instead of rushing right into this life-changing commitment (like I usually do), I decided to make a few calls to see what I'd be getting myself into. After all, my current job is boring but it does provide a company car, an expense account, mileage, a monthly uniform allowance, health care benefits and two weeks of vacation; things I'm sure aren't included in being a freelance sperm donor.

The first step toward financial freedom as a sperm donor is to find a reputable sperm bank; sort of like finding the right talent agent. A good sperm bank will take care of everything: the donor screening, specimen collections as well as banking sperm for future distribution. While this isn't quite as easy as opening a new saving account at Wells Fargo, with the resources on the Internet, it's not that difficult, either.

Because I live in a remote area of Colorado, the closest sperm bank that I could find was CryoGam Colorado, LLC in Loveland. They had a very professional web page that provided straightforward information on the entire process.

To be eligible to be a sperm donor, men need to be between 18 and 35 years of age, in good physical health, free from all of the usual diseases (HIV, AIDS, STD's, genital warts, herpes, Ebola, leprosy, typhus, cholera, tuberculosis, dysentery, Grocer's Itch, scurvy and ringworm) and be able to provide a complete health history of their family, going back as far as the 14th century. Most sperm banks like you to be either a college graduate or attending college at the time of application; preferably a Doctorate program in one of the Ivy League schools. Since I have an MFA in Comparative Ceramics from the California College of Arts and Crafts, I felt that my educational credentials would be more than adequate.

After you've completed all of the paperwork and returned it in a plain, brown envelope, it's time to come in and make your first preliminary "deposit."

Before I was considered a card-carrying sperm donor, I'd be required to make a series of three "introductory offers" to test my sperm for viability, so it's off to the Masturbatorium I go. Specifically, they're looking for sperm count, motility (how fast my boys can swim), how well my sperm freeze, thaw and morphology, or general characteristics. I was informed that only 20-50% of all applicants get past the first audition: odds just a little better than landing a starring role on Broadway.

Assuming that I'd be asked back for a second audition, I'd need to volunteer a second and third sample; the operative word being "volunteer." So, it's off to the Masturbatorium again. Up to this point, I still wasn't being paid for my service to the community. I was still trying out for the team. And making the team has its own set of responsibilities: I wouldn't be allowed to make any "unauthorized withdrawals" for anyone, including myself, at least three to five days prior to each donation. Hmmm . . .

Next, came the physical examination. During this phase, I was poked and prodded for ABO-Rh blood typing, complete blood count (CBC), full chemistry panel, cystic fibrosis carrier screening, semen analysis, sickle cell and Tay-Sachs carrier testing and a urinalysis. If I was lucky enough to make the cut, I'd be rewarded by more invasive tests for ALT, Chlamydia, gonorrhea, hepatitis B, hepatitis C, HIV and syphilis. Lucky me.

After successfully passing the physical examination and health history, I sat around and waited to see if I made the team. I imagined a scene you'd see on ESPN during the NFL draft picks—being surrounded on the couch with all of my relatives and closest friends, waiting for the telephone to ring informing me that I had been chosen in the first round by CryoGam for their starting lineup. I just got an envelope in the mail.

Once I agreed to sign the contract for "Wankers Anonymous," I was required to adhere to a number of very specific guidelines and requests; after all this is a business. These include consenting that I have absolutely no legal responsibility to any child that is conceived from my sperm, I have no rights to the child and that I will remain anonymous—just about everything a player in the NBA is looking for as he's running around the country sowing his wild oats.

I found out later that once I signed the agreement, I'd have to commit to CryoGam for six months to three years of service. I would be restricted to providing less than 10 children from my sperm, although there have been a number of cases contesting this. One donor was refuted to have provided sperm for more than 450 children. But, he was a professional with years of experience, claimed he needed the money to get his car out of the shop and didn't care how painful it was to walk. Many states have strict laws governing consanguinity.

Finally, the matter of money. Although arrangements vary from one sperm bank to the next, I was told that I could count on earning around $50.00

per specimen, plus $5.00 for each vial that was taken from my specimen. Since most specimens yield 10-14 vials per specimen, I could make as much as $200.00 per specimen. Of course, this is before taxes, so right off the bat, CryoGam took the wind out of my "sales" and pointed me toward the proper IRS forms. As far as I can remember, this was the first time in my life I'd have to pay taxes for masturbating.

After I finished evaluating all of the requirements, I ultimately decided to pass on the opportunity. I like being able to take liberties with myself whenever I'm struck with the urge—and my girlfriend was getting jealous because the lab was getting all of the good stuff.

Let's Get This Potty Started

I was in my early 20s, when I decided to take a break from the tedious life I had created for myself and spend a summer in Munich, Germany. Ever since I saw Leni Riefenstahl's epic documentary of the 1938 Olympic Games, I wanted to experience for myself what it would be like to pole vault in Bavaria.

With barely $500 to live on, I realized that I'd need some way to support myself, so I hit the straße looking for work. After several days, the only thing I could come up with was an administrative job in the United States Army Post Exchange Headquarters. It wasn't the greatest job I've ever had and certainly didn't satisfy my desire to be immersed in German track and field, but it paid for my round trip airfare, and still left a little spare time to explore southern Germany on the weekends.

One day, during the height of our busiest season, my American co-workers and I began to notice how much time the German nationals were taking for "restroom breaks," leaving us with the lion share of the work. Since it's pretty hard to argue with someone over their hygienic practices, I wrote an fictitious memo from the Commander of the Post Exchange System to get deadbeats thinking before taking their 10th restroom break of the day. I forged the Commander's signature, printed the memo on official letterhead and distributed it throughout the Exchange Headquarters. It read something like this:

From: Colonel John Wittenberg, Commander, United States Army Post Exchange System
To: All employees of United States Army Post Exchange System Administrative Headquarters, Munich, Germany.

Subject: New Schedule for Restroom Breaks

It has come to the attention of the Commander of the Army Post Exchange System that some staff members may be taking unfair advantage of our liberal schedule for visiting the restroom. Up until this time, the Commander has allowed unlimited visits, with little or no accounting for time lost during the workday when employees use the facilities. After auditing the amount of lost time spent in the restroom, a number of corrective measures will be put in place to bring the Army Post Exchange System back in line with similar units in other divisions of the armed forces.

Beginning on Monday, August 7, 1972, visits to the restrooms will be metered out with a maximum of ten minutes per visit per employee—one visit in the morning and one in the afternoon. Each visit begins the moment the employee leaves their desk and ends when they return. It includes travel time to and from the facilities and time spent waiting for the elevators. The schedule is as follows:

Last name beginning with the letter:	A.M. restroom visit time:
A—D	0800—0810
E—H	0810—0820
I—L	0820—0830
M—P	0830—0840
Q—T	0840—0850
U—Z	0850—0900
Lunchtime	**Facilities closed**
Last name beginning with the letter:	**P.M. restroom visit time:**
A—D	1300—1310
E—H	1310—1320
I—L	1320—1330
M—P	1330—1340
Q—T	1340—1350
U—Z	1350—1400

In addition to the liberal visitation schedule, you are required to observe the following guidelines:

- Each employee is allowed only two restroom visits per day—one in the morning and one in the afternoon. Requests for additional visits will be denied unless accompanied with a note from their doctor.

- If an employee misses their scheduled morning visit, they forfeit that visit and must wait until their afternoon time.

- Employees are free to exchange their scheduled visit times with other employees having different last names. All exchanges must be approved by the department manager three days in advance of the requested visit.

- Employees are granted three additional, non-scheduled visits per month that may be banked for emergencies such as excessive caffeine consumption, diarrhea or dealing with the after effects of Oktoberfest.

- Each restroom visit is limited to a total of 5 minutes and begins the moment the employee enters or exits the restroom.

- Men and women may not use each other's facilities if the others' is full.

- Employees must have their thumbprints scanned for entry into the stalls.

- The stall doors will not open if the employee is not using the facilities within their approved time.

- Employees are allowed three sheets of toilet paper per visit and will show up as a line item deduction on their bi-weekly paycheck at 5 cents per sheet.

- Employees are allowed a maximum of 3 ½ minutes to use the stalls. Once the maximum time has passed, the stall doors will automatically spring open, an alarm will go off and their photograph will be taken.

- Employees who exceed their allotted time will have their photographs posted in the hallways as people who habitually ignore company policies.

- Employees whose photos are posted three times will be suspended from work for two weeks without pay and be required to attend a two-hour Policies and Procedures class on how to properly use the restrooms.

We're excited about the new policies and hope you will be too. They should result in a more efficient workplace for all. If you have any questions regarding the new policies, please contact your manager at their home after 9:00 P.M. Thank you.

I Want To Take You: Hire

According to recent statistics, over 13.5 million Americans were pulled, kicking and screaming into the ranks of the unemployed this year. Unlike other organizations to which I've belonged, I didn't even want to become a member. I didn't attend a free introductory seminar, I wasn't sponsored by another associate, nor was I coaxed into joining with the promise of a free condo in Aspen. In fact, I'd have to say that I've gone to almost any length to achieve expulsion.

Ten years ago, I found myself in a similar situation. After a couple of weeks off for R & R, I perused the Internet, applied for three or four interesting positions and made a few telephone calls on Monday morning. A couple of interviews later, I'm sitting behind a new desk with a grin on my face, filling out health insurance forms and deciding what position to play on the company softball team. Thirteen months of continuous unemployment suggests to me that this time, it was going to be different.

Fortunately, there is no shortage of help available to the unemployed. Immediately upon hearing of my plight, well-wishing friends began descending on me with anecdotes on how they landed their first job 30 years ago at El Taco Grande. Websites abound with information addressing every conceivable angle of the job hunt from writing Pulitzer Prize winning cover letters to preparing for an interview. But the first and most time honored tactic is scanning the want ads.

In their despair to screen for the best applicants, corporations have begun writing want ads with almost impossible qualifications. For instance, I ran across this one last week:

Certified Public Accountant.

Large metropolitan accounting firm seeks tri-lingual Rhodes Scholar to join dynamic group of plumbing auditors for the California Division of Corrections. Must have 3-5 years of experience in nuclear physics, international fund raising, IBM mainframe system design and be willing to travel 350 days a year using their own car without reimbursement. Must possess a concealed weapon permit, black belt in Tae Kwan Do and current Idaho Cosmetology license. Ability to work well in dark, cramped and moist environments a definite plus. Please forward resume, salary history, recent urinalysis and stool specimen to: Ms. Petunia Plotnik, Director of Circular Filing, 13568 East 456th Street North, West Los Angeles, CA 90017. EOE

Writing a good resume is essential to getting a job—even one you don't want. And while there are many ways to go about creating one, a resume is really nothing more than standing up in front of class and telling the other students what you did last summer. It should be clear and concise so the interviewer knows what you've been up to since Moses descended Mount Sinai. Never lie. Find creative ways to explain any gaps in your employment. For instance, instead of writing "Served 3 to 5 years at Rikers Island for armed robbery," replace it with, "1997-1999 Participated in a federally funded men's retreat."

After five weeks of futile searching, I threw in the towel and resorted to professional help. Recruiters or "headhunters" as they're often called, promote the façade that after one 15-minute meeting, they can line up the interview that has successfully eluded you your entire life. This may be true if you have certain marketable skills in "hot" career tracks, such as sushi wrapping, karma repair or zither tuning. But if you're a college educated professional with current technical expertise, you'll be treated with all of the hospitality of a telemarketer calling at suppertime. But don't give up. There is still one more indispensable resource available to you: the unemployment office.

Unemployment offices are called many things: the Employment Development Department, the Department of Labor or the Department

63

of Labor and Employment (as opposed to the Department of No Labor and Unemployment). The DLE is the black hole of the universe. People walk in and are never seen or heard from again.

Before you do business with the DLE, there are a few things you might as well accept from the beginning. First, no matter which form you complete, it will always be the wrong one, so be prepared to go back to the end of the line at least three or four times. In preparation for the inevitable, I always fill out one of every form in the rack and let the clerks take their pick. Second, be prepared to wait. During my last visit, I sat next to a gentleman who had fallen asleep under a newspaper dated April 6, 1965. I knew I was in for a long wait. Finally, if you have any advanced education, don't expect much help in finding work through the DLE. Dead giveaways are the category headings for available positions: Part-time Sewer Technicians and Taco Bell "Team Members." The DLE is usually one of the last resources that the Brookings Institution depends on for filling vacancies. But, assuming that you do find someone who will grant you an interview, you still have a lot of work ahead of you.

I've always been able to accurately predict when an important interview is imminent: a new pimple the size of Mount Vesuvius has erupted on the tip of my nose and my dog has just chewed off the left leg of my best suit. Nonetheless, it's important to prepare for interviews by going over in your mind how you'll respond to certain well-worn interview questions.

My favorite interview question has always been: "Describe for me your greatest accomplishment within the last five years." What immediately comes to mind is playing the 'Star Spangled Banner' by cupping my hand under my armpit. Given the circumstances, however, I usually come up with the vapid, rehearsed response, "I coordinated and implemented a multi-factorial, time-sharing system for database decentralization and integrated modular output using C++." The most unfair question you'll get (and everybody gets it) is: "Describe to me your greatest weakness". Right. As if I'm actually going to admit to taking 35 sick days last year. And there was, of course, that minor issue in the ladies' room . . . But instead, I reflexively gaze up to the ceiling and respond with the standard, "Well, gee. I don't know. I suppose if I do have a weakness, its being too honest at times." They always love that one.

The hardest part of the entire process comes immediately after the interview: the waiting period. It's one of the few times during your search for work that laying on the couch, doing nothing is condoned. This, of course, perpetuates the internal argument: should I call them, or wait until they call me? I want to appear professional, but not too anxious. So, if I make up my mind to call, how long should I wait before picking up the phone? Is seven days too many? Four days too few? I haven't experienced this much internal conflict since dating in high school.

Finally, the call comes. My last interviewer wants to begin checking my references. So I email them a carefully prepared list of the few remaining people that will vouch for me. These are people that still owe me money or haven't seen me in over 12 years. A few of them are dead. And then I wait some more . . .

Over the course of the last 30 years, I estimate that I've worked more than 60,000 hours. I've served donuts, tacos, weenies, burgers and fries. I've driven ice cream trucks, forklifts, go-carts, vans and trams. I've worked inside, outside, morning, noon and night. I love having a job. Sometimes, I can't believe that it's so hard to find something that so many other people don't want. Anybody hiring?

Daring Dining

Entertaining out of town guests can be difficult. Especially when it comes to finding original, trendy places to dine. After all, once you've had one surf & turf, you've had them all. Fortunately, the food and beverage industry is never at a loss for new and unusual places to eat. Here's a list of my favorite new restaurants. Admittedly, I haven't been to them all, but they're on my bucket list.

The Heart Attack Grill—Dallas, Texas and Chandler, Arizona
The Heart Attack Grill makes no apologies for its menu. In fact, every featured item embraces an unhealthy diet. Located in Chandler, Arizona and Dallas, Texas, the Heart Attack Grill includes items like the Single, Double, Triple and Quadruple Bypass Burgers that can contain as much as two pounds of beef and over 8,000 calories. Accompany your burger with an order of Flatliner Fries (cooked in pure lard), a pure Butterfat Shake or a tall glass of full sugar Coca-Cola® and you'll be well on your way to heart disease. As an added bonus, anyone who finishes a Quadruple Bypass Burger receives a free ride to their car in a wheelchair.

Cannibalistic Sushi—Tokyo, Japan
If you think that once you've eaten at one sushi restaurant, you've eaten at them all, you're in for a surprise. The staff at Cannibalistic Sushi begins by wheeling in a female body made of dough to your table. The body contains organs that are made from a delicious selection of sushi items. The hostess begins your dining experience by splaying open the body's chest with a scalpel, then inviting patrons to "dig in."

Modern Toilet—Taipei, Taiwan
For many people, décor is as important as the menu in the overall dining experience. Embracing that belief, Modern Toilet seats hungry guests on western-style commodes and uses rolls of toilet paper instead of napkins.

Drinks are served in miniature urinals and guests can enjoy a wide variety of offerings, including feces-shaped chocolate soft serve.

Pitch Black Restaurant—Beijing, China
If you're looking for a dimly lit, intimate dining experience to impress your first date, then the Pitch Black Restaurant is for you. Diners eat in total darkness—so dark, you can't see your hand in front of your face. Waiters wearing night vision goggles bring your food to your table and help you to find the plate that's sitting directly in your lap.

Alcatraz ER—Tokyo, Japan
Everyone enjoys good hospital food. And, for those who want the best, Alcatraz ER couples the sterility of a hospital with the feeling of confinement at the famous federal penitentiary. The evening begins by scantily clad "nurses" handcuffing you to their wrist while transporting you to your cell. While sitting in captivity, you can order delicacies like Dead Chicken, Penis Sausage and intestines.

Cereality—Dallas-Fort Worth, Texas; Mankato, Minnesota; Dayton, Ohio and Morgantown, West Virginia
For those of you who love breakfast at any time of the day, you'll love the concept behind Cereality. Founded by two entrepreneurs who just love a good bowl of cereal, Cereality feels instantly familiar. Walk up to the counter and you can order items off the "Our Way" menu, like "PB & Crunch," "Life's a Bowl of Cherries," "Flak n' Out," or "S'More Than You Know." Or, you can order from the "Your Way" menu by combining any one of more than 14 types of cereal like Fruit Loops, Cheerios, Frosted Mini Wheats and Raisin Bran, topped off with almonds, blueberries, crushed Oreo cookies, pecans, raisins and many others—23 in all. Cereality also caters events and sells U.S. franchises.

Buns and Guns—Beirut, Lebanon
Diners interested in a more military experience will love the food and décor of Buns and Guns. Patterned around Lebanon's 2006 War with Israel, guests enjoy menu items like the M16 Carbine sandwich, the Mortar Burger or Terrorist Meal, while the constant drone of helicopters and land mine explosions blare loudly overhead.

Cabbages & Condoms—Bangkok, Thailand

Cabbages & Condoms is a unique dining experience that is a joint effort between private interests and the Population and Community Development Association, dedicated to promoting birth control. Featuring menu items like Spicy Condom Salad, the restaurant offers exiting guests condoms instead of breath mints.

Hobbit House—Manila, Philippines

Advocates of political correctness may want to think twice before eating at the Hobbit House. Founded by a former Peace Corps volunteer and J.R.R. Tolkien fan, the Hobbit House is staffed by the smallest waiters in the world.

Dinner in the Sky—Las Vegas, Nevada

Just when you think that Las Vegas has conquered every unique experience on earth, along comes Dinner in the Sky. Suspended over 180 feet in the air on a clear Plexiglas floor, 22 diners enjoy some of the most spectacular views of the gambling empire, while dining on fine food prepared and served by Sky Chefs. For $289, each guest is picked up and dropped off at their hotel, enjoys a red carpet reception and a complimentary photograph, memorializing the evening. Guests must be at least four feet tall and weigh less than 300 pounds. Visits to the restroom are discouraged.

Rising Sun Anger Release Bar—Nanjing City, China

If a good, stiff drink (or two) fails to help you deal with the stress of a day at the office, then perhaps punching one of the staff at the Rising Sun Anger Release Bar could be the ticket. Customers pay an entrance fee at the door, then are free to yell, throw glasses, degrade and beat up the staff. Members of the staff wear specially designed protective equipment and will even dress up to resemble the person you'd really like to pulverize (your boss?). The bar is said to be particularly popular with Chinese women in the service industry.

Dick's Last Resort—Petco Park, California, Las Vegas, Nevada and other locations

People who enjoy a five-star dining experience and staff catering to their every needs should go somewhere else than Dick's Last Resort. Famous for its memorable dining décor of picnic tables and no tablecloths, Dick's hires only obnoxious servers who throw your napkins and utensils at you, while spewing forth insults. Diners wear "bibs," or paper hats to wear through the meal, that they can emblazon with insults like, "Member of the Manson family," "I'm wearing Hannah Montana's underwear," "Accepting hair donations here," "Retired Pole Dancer" and "I'm so old, I fart dust."

So, regardless of where you live, there's always a new and unusual place for you to insult your friends, relatives and guests at the dinner table. Be bold. Be creative. But, above all, be daring!

The Sedentary Life

It's that dreaded time of the year again. Time for my annual physical. And since I haven't followed any of the suggestions Doctor Sphinctergard made last year, it's a pretty safe bet that I can look forward to dismal news again. After spending an entire morning in his office being stripped, squeezed, poked and prodded, he'll tell me that I'm overweight, hypertensive, pre-diabetic, sedentary, near sighted, weak, losing my sight, hearing, smell, taste, touch and most of my hair. And that's before any of the lab results come back.

It's no mystery why I'm in the condition that I am. According to health and fitness experts, the adult metabolism declines approximately 1% per year between the ages of 25 and 50. That means that within the first year after graduation from college, I started my downward plunge into lethargy until I reached middle age—then I really started to stack on the pounds. Of course, sitting in a cubicle for a quarter of my life looking at a computer screen didn't help. Neither did three pieces of birthday cake every Friday afternoon.

Sure enough, Doctor Sphinctergard came back into the examination room, shaking his head, as I started slipping out of my hospital gown. The bad news: I was going to have to start exercising.

It's not that I have anything against exercising. Some of my best friends like to sweat. It's just that I have so many good reasons not to. For one thing, exercising makes me hot, sweaty and it's embarrassing how my fat jiggles around when I run. It's also boring, makes my feet smell and is tough to do when I'm hung-over. Not only that, it's almost impossible to keep a cigarette lit while you're jogging. Then there's all that additional laundry to keep up with. Despite all of these good reasons, Doctor Sphinctergard wasn't going to take no for an answer. This year I was going to get fit.

To help me gather momentum, I hired a personal trainer to assist with the impossible: keep me moving for longer than two weeks. I found Thigbe listed in Craigslist and asked him to work with me because of his success with celebrities like Dusti Swetman, Wanda Gay Hamilton, Edward Jump and Academy Award winner Leota Stoo-Olanda when she had to drop all of that weight to play Akeakamai in "The Spinalonga Leprosy Story." If he could help them, he could help me.

Thigbe came over one afternoon so we could design a plan for keeping me active. My goal was to weigh what I did in high school by January 1st using methods other than liposuction and limb amputation. "You have to begin by choosing things you like to do," said Thigbe. "Let's start with activities you did successfully in high school or college." I told him forty years ago I was a pretty good pole vaulter, hammer thrower and held three records in the 3000 meter steeplechase, triple-jump, javelin and 400 meter hurdles but given the constraints of living in a condominium complex, I didn't think it would be a good idea to start my new program by pole vaulting into my neighbor's yard or throwing the javelin into their bedroom. I could probably steeplechase over their rose bushes, though. Ultimately, I opted to leave it up to Thigbe.

The first obstacle that I hadn't anticipated was buying all new exercise clothing. My 1973 Adidas track suit was impossible to fit into and the crotch had been eaten away by moths. But it did have a handy pocket for my cigarettes and lighter. So I headed to Walmart to find a replacement.

Chu Mi Goo was very helpful in helping me pick out what I needed. He asked me what I enjoyed: Yoga? Pilates? Tae Kwan Do? Tai Chi? or was I planning on Wii in the comfort of my own home? I told Chu that my nutritionist was going to talk with me later about my diet. Right now, I just needed some comfortable clothes for walking and jogging. I also needed some new footwear. Being limited on funds I decided on a pair of multi-sport ice-climbing boots with stainless steel studs in the soles: something that was durable and would work well for walking, running, archery, field hockey, golf, hunting, lacrosse, paintball, skateboarding, snowboarding, soccer and tennis. They wouldn't work very well for figure skating, hockey, in-line skating, skiing, snorkeling, surfing, swimming or water polo but I'd deal with that when the time came.

Thigbe told me that we'd start our first session tomorrow morning at 5:30 sharp—before my anti-depressants wore off and long before it dawned on me what I was doing to myself. There are a lot of other advantages to working out early in the morning. First, no one is around to make fun of how silly your hair looks. Second, it's too early for anything to get in the way, like making a living or catching up on your Tweets. And third, the streets are free of student drivers, so there's a good chance that you won't get smeared along the side of the highway before you get back home.

Thigbe said he had designed the perfect program for me that was patterned after his Navy Seal training. Guaranteed to get results. We'd start slowly and work our way up to optimum fitness by the end of the year. After some brief stretching, he screamed at me to hit the deck and crank out 35 one-armed push-ups while he kept his foot pressed on the back of my neck. This was followed by 30 minutes of crawling around in the street gutters with a wooden rifle, slithering underneath the parked cars, followed by rappelling down the side of the International House of Pancakes where he allowed me to eat breakfast while jogging in place. After breakfast, he chased me back home in his Hummer and made me get dressed without taking a shower before heading for the office. That was day one.

Day two with Thigbe never came. I called him that night and thanked him for his expertise, but I was interested in something a little less demanding. After he muttered a few choice words—something about where my mother was born—we parted ways and I started my search for a health club.

After scouring the yellow pages, I found the Memorial Fitness Center ten minutes from home. I was a little concerned about the Center having the same type of name as a cemetery, but I decided to give it try anyway. I walked up to the reception desk and asked what they had in affordable fitness programs. "Are you interested in Yoga? Pilates? Tae Kwan Do? or Tai Chi?" asked the receptionist. Again with the food. "No, my nutritionist is going to talk with me later about my diet. I'd just like to get started with some light pole vaulting and hammer throwing." She ran to get the manager.

As a new member of the Memorial Fitness Center, I was entitled to one free session with a personal trainer. Jeanne-Hélène introduced herself and suggested that we start with a ten minute warm-up, so she had me jump up on a treadmill facing a dozen flat screen televisions—all tuned to the Food Channel. After watching Paula Deen, Rachel Ray and Guy Fieri whip up one dessert after another, I was famished, so I headed to the snack bar for a stack of blueberry pancakes and a vente Caramel Brulee Frappuccino.

I wandered back into the fitness center and found Jeanne-Hélène patiently waiting for me in the free weight room. "Since it's been a while since you've done anything, we're going to start you out on a simple weight training routine designed to improve your overall fitness." That translated to, "You're so fat and out of shape, I'm going to have you do next to nothing so I don't have to worry about giving you a heart attack and lose my job."

"I've selected a number of popular exercises for you," she said. "Watson Flys, Hammarstrom Curls, Luquiens Lunges, Brisbane Extensions and Slaqboom Sit-ups. Later, we'll add a few Wadsworth Presses, Carnwath Squats, Fangel Snatches and Gaugengigl Raises." I didn't know what any of those were but they sounded like they'd work.

After Jeanne-Hélène demonstrated each of the exercises, she had me give them a go. I was feeling fitter already. At the end of the hour, we parted ways and I headed back to the snack bar for a Cheeseburger Smoothie and a cigarette.

The next morning I was in mortal pain. Every ligament, tendon, fascia and bursa objected to even the slightest movement. After mustering enough energy to call in sick for the day, I laid in bed confident that I had not only found another reason not to exercise, but a bonafide excuse to load up on prescription painkillers. Enduring this much pain just wasn't for me. I'd rather be fat and sedentary with no will power.

Thankfully I have an entire year before I have to look Doctor Sphinctergard in the eye.

Speed Dating Cougars, MILFs and Chihuahuas

Ten minutes after my divorce was final, I decided that I'd waited long enough to go looking for the woman of my dreams. Or, at least the next woman of my dreams. The first one was the sausage jockey I left in 1973 after I came home early and caught her playing "Twister" in the buff with the UPS driver.

I heard from my friends that dating in the 21st Century might be a tad different than I remember it. Guys don't cruise the boulevard looking for chicks at the malt shop anymore and it's not cool to leave large hickies on their necks. So, I decided to do some research before I got busy.

The Internet has made dating infinitely easier than it used to be. Thanks to my Comcast account, there's no longer any need to shower and stumble up to my date's front door with sweaty palms. I can cut right to the chase from the comfort of my Lazy Boy while eating Doritos in my underwear. Through the wonders of online dating, I can pretend to be anyone I want to be—just like all of the divorced Betties spending their Friday nights glued to the computer screen.

There are thousands of helpful articles to help you navigate the world of cyber-necking. Online dating is safer and easier than traditional dating because you never have to worry about actually coming into physical contact with people. By the time they've figured out who you really are, they've probably already taken out a temporary restraining order against you, blacklisted your email address and disabled their cell phone.

Before you start dating, you need to learn some important terms. These are expressions that never existed the last time I was single. If you're a woman, you'll probably run across the term, "Boy Toy." Boy Toys are younger dates for older women who are used exclusively for sexual gratification and enjoyment. I might have been someone's Boy Toy years ago but I didn't know it at the time. Boy Toys are frequently targeted by "Cougars." A Cougar is a woman in her 40s, 50s or 60s who stalks younger men in their 20s. I know it's hard to believe, but I'm told they really do exist.

"MILFs" are "mothers I'd like to @#$%." The term was popularized in the film, "American Pie" and fills thousands of sites on the Internet. If you don't believe me, just have your pubescent son Google "older women" for his next sociology report. Other important terms are "Jailbait," "Lolita," "Sugar Daddy," "Sugar Momma," "Chihuahua" and "May-December romance." You can even combine them. For instance, last week I thought I had a date with a MILF, but she turned out to be a Cougar Sugar Momma who was after a Boy Toy for a May-December romance.

If you've found that you just can't meet anyone your age and would like to explore older or younger partners, you can use the handy "half-your-age-plus-7" rule. It's a simple mathematical equation that's designed to help you judge the social acceptance of intimate relationships between two, age-disparate, consulting adults. The equation states:

Age of Younger Individual > (Age of the older individual/2) + 7

If numbers aren't your thing, you can use the handy half-your-age-plus-7graph available on the Internet to determine who's within your age range. According to the graph, I should be compatible with any woman between 35 and 120. That means I can look forward to dating either a woman racing through her sexual prime or one who's cleared the hurdles of menopause over 70 years ago.

I also learned some valuable terms when it comes to members of the opposite sex. Men don't refer to women as "dolls" or "babes" anymore. Today, they're either an "Aunt Jemima," "Aviation Blonde," "Bad Kitty," "Becky," "Betty," "Bimbo," "Bimho," "Buffy," "Chank," "Chicken Head," "Dime," "Grizzly Chicken," "Hockey Whore," "Hoochie Mamma," "Hose Beast," "Jumpoff," "Pebbles," "Puck Bunny," "Skank," "Space Queen" or a "Yummy Mummy." A man could be a "Baldwin," "Mack Daddy," "Mimbo," "Scrub," "Spider" or a "Thoroughbred."

If you feel your biological clock racing, you may want to accelerate things by trying speed dating. This technique was invented by Rabbi Yaacov Deyo as a way for Jewish singles to meet people and was popularized on the hit television show, "Sex and the City." At most speed dating functions, women are seated at a table and the men rotate between the stations until they've met each woman. Each "date" lasts only 7-minutes, so there's not a lot of room for small talk. After each 7-minute date, both participants jot down on a card whether or not they'd be interested in meeting one another again. The results are tallied by the event organizer and after he's finished hitting on all of the attractive women, he'll forward the leftovers to the participants who've indicated that they'd be up for stomaching another 7-minute date. Maybe even longer.

Speed dating is the equivalent of getting to know someone, using a Tivo—you can fast forward through a dozen men or women in a single evening. Of course its main limitation is it doesn't allow you to experience the most thrilling parts of traditional dating: fear, rejection and resentment. It's popular with singles between 30 and 45 because most of them haven't as yet felt the exhilaration of losing their homes, Corvette, mobile home, ski cabin, bank account and business to their ex as she rides away on the back of a Harley with her new mimbo. One enterprising manager of a retirement home tried organizing a speed dating event for seniors, but by the time they shuffled between tables dragging their oxygen tanks, they only met two people in an hour. Personally, I've only speed dated once. While sprinting between tables, I pulled a hamstring and had to be carted away by paramedics. By the time my physical therapist released me for action, I'd lost the urge to continue dating.

Another great way to meet someone is by forming a relationship at work. Marriage experts estimate that more than 70% of men and women who meet at work are still married after 10 years. One of the advantages of being introduced at work is that you can get to know the real person under the most difficult circumstances before you make any commitments. If you still find your partner attractive after watching them pummel the jammed photocopier or stealing office supplies, chances are you'll be able to put up with the rest of their antics after you're married.

Many "sunset singles" who have finally met the man or women of their dreams, decide to forgo getting married in favor of "living apart together," or LAT. LAT relationships let two people date and consider themselves a couple, while maintaining separate residences. It's a win-win situation for both—he can keep all of his old pornographic VHS tapes and she can continue sliding into bed, slathered in cold cream.

Once you've finally met someone you want to grow old with, you're still not home free. You'll have to meet all of their children, grandchildren, great-grandchildren, brothers, sisters, cousins, their housekeeper, personal assistant, therapist, live-in maid, gastroenterologist, cardiologist, anesthesiologist, dermatologist, gerontologist, hematologist, hepatologist, immunologist, neurologist, ophthalmologist, oral surgeon, pathologist, podiatrist, psychiatrist, pulmonologist, radiologist, rheumatologist, serologist, toxicologist and urologist. Then, you'll have to learn about all of their special needs and the dozens of medications they take on a daily basis.

At this point, I can see that dating again isn't going to be nearly as much fun as the first time around. I might be better off staying single and continuing to lie about myself on Match.com.

Maneuvering Through M&Ms

I'm the kind of person who can go their entire life without telling someone what to do. Call me lazy or lackadaisical, I just think anyone over the age of 12 should have enough sense to do the right thing—like moving their shopping cart out of the way when they run over to the next aisle to grab the pickles they forgot.

Apparently though, I stand alone on this subject, so I suppose I'll have to take this opportunity to expound on the way supermarkets *should* be run—through my four-point plan for supermarket and shopper regulation.

Point one would require all shoppers to be at least 21 years of age to operate a shopping cart. In certain states, (California, Kentucky, Illinois and Hawaii) learner's permits could be issued six months prior to turning 21. The permit holder would be limited to operating a shopping cart during daylight hours with a licensed adult over 21 seat-belted into the passenger's seat.

All applicants would be required to pass a 300-question written examination every year, addressing the rules for safe shopping cart operation. Some sample test questions might include the following:

1. **When approaching an unattended cart in the center of an aisle, you should do which of the following?**
   a) Wait patiently until the shopper returns and moves their cart
   b) Push the cart into the parking lot without telling the owner
   c) Ram the cart out of the way
   d) None of the above

2. **After arriving at the check stand, you observe that the shopper in front of you failed to push their cart through the line. Therefore, you should do which of the following:**
   a) Repeatedly bump them from behind to call attention to their oversight
   b) Lift their cart up onto the conveyor belt and let the checker deal with it
   c) Scoop armloads of candy and Hollywood tabloids onto the end of their order
   d) Ask them if this was an oversight, or has there been a city-wide ban on good manners

3. **You come to the intersection of the dairy case and a Doritos display. There are two elderly women chatting, preventing you from making a safe left-hand turn. What should you do?**
   a) Make a U-turn and go down another aisle to avoid being detained
   b) Bulldoze them out of the way and apologize after you're clear
   c) Ask them to take you to the aisle where the Polident is located
   d) Tell them that their shuttle-bus to the retirement home has just left

After successfully completing the written examination, the licensee-in-training would then be eligible to take the driving test. Applicants would have to demonstrate proficiency in extricating a cart from the phalanx at the front of the store using one hand. They would be required to demonstrate defensive driving skills while maneuvering through a minefield of M&Ms scattered on the floor. Deductions would be made for sideswiping other carts or driving down the wrong side of the aisle.

The final part of the practical test would require a demonstration of safe cart handling under extreme conditions. The applicant should be able to demonstrate that they can keep their shopping cart on a straight trajectory, while their kids pull cookies, candy and Yoo-Hoo off of the shelves.

Point Two would address proper shopping cart maintenance and equipment regulations. Prospective licensees would be required to identify the major components of a cart, change a flat tire and repair a jiggling front wheel, while keeping a safe distance from on-coming traffic. The new regulations would also gradually phase-out shopping carts as supermarket property.

By the year 2015, all shoppers would be required to purchase their own carts and transport them to the market on specially designed automobile roof racks. Personal carts would have to comply with state regulations for height, weight, width, turning radius, road clearance and maximum hauling capacity. Optional equipment such as off road suspension, 4-wheel drive (including manually locking front hubs), halogen fog lamps, THX sound systems, roll bars, CD players, air shock lift kits, custom bed liners, ABS braking systems, running boards, customized passenger compartments and tires wider that 24 inches would have to be approved by state inspection stations prior to being allowed to enter the store.

Shopping cart insurance would be sold as additional riders onto standard automobile insurance policies to cover damage that occurred inside the supermarkets. Premiums would be based on age, sex, history of moving violations, geographical location of supermarket and model and year of shopping cart. Naturally, more expensive premiums would be assessed to high performance sport-utility carts (SUCs) and carts without theft deterrent systems.

Point Three would address moving violations, definitions for infractions and penalties. Although regulated by the state, each supermarket would employ their own traffic enforcement officials. Affectionately known as "Melon Heads," they would routinely patrol the aisles, concentrating on particularly high-risk areas. Melon Heads would issue citations for infractions like shopping in the wrong direction, holding the freezer door open for more than 10 seconds, illegal aisle changes and shopping while under the influence of children. The following is a list of common infractions followed by their accompanying penalties:

Infraction # 5001, Open ice cream container in cart

Penalty: Offender must attend 28-day substance abuse program and pay $10,000

Infraction # 2113, Illegal aisle change
Penalty: Offender must leave cart outside and use hand basket for 10 days

Infraction # 1717, Excessive speed
Penalty: Offender must shop with their shoelaces tied together for no less than 6 months

Infraction # 7856, Grand theft cart
Penalty: Offender is admonished to shop at 7-Elevens and Loaf & Jug stores for no less than 12 months

Infraction # 3117, Shopping too slowly
Penalty: Offender is only allowed to enter store during the last 10 minutes before closing

Depending on the severity of the infraction, the typical penalties for first-timers would range from shopping while handcuffed to a court-appointed officer to mandatory attendance of Safe Shoppers School. However, repeat offenders would be dealt the heavy hand of the law. Adhering to the "Three strikes and you're out" policy, those found to be habitual violators would be sentenced to serve 12 months as Walmart greeters.

Point Four would govern the construction and operation of the supermarket facility. All supermarket designs would be certified by the state government to include the following criteria:

1. Each market must have a maximum of 3 unlabeled entrances and exits. Only one has to function properly at a time.
2. Each aisle can be no more than 1.5 times the width of a regulation shopping cart. This does not include promotional displays that project from the shelves and catch on clothing
3. The temperature of the ice cream section should be no less than 5 degrees cooler than the temperature outside the store.

4. The produce misters must be equipped with motion detectors, set to effuse a fine spray on unsuspecting shoppers whenever they reach for items on the back of the produce table.

5. Supermarkets must utilize special, pressure-sensitive floor plates to monitor the length of checkout lines. Whenever the line exceeds 3 customers, 2 checkers at alternative stations would be required to cash out and take their lunch without being replaced.

In addition to the previously mentioned points, shoppers would no longer be free to wander from aisle to aisle in a haphazard fashion. All shoppers would be required to enter the supermarket through the right-hand entrance. Tri-colored traffic lights would allow one shopper in at a time, based on the number of shoppers exiting the store.

Once inside, the shoppers would be required to push their carts in a counter-clockwise direction around the perimeter of the store. If they need to turn down one of the center aisles, they would do so using only left-hand turns. If the shopper forgets an item, they would be required to make a complete circuit around the store until they were in position to make a legal, left-hand turn.

I'm not really sure what I can do single-handedly to improve the quality of our shopping experience. At the very least, I'm going to fold up this article and jam it into the store's suggestion box. Maybe they'll get the message.

I'm Loathing It

One of the best things about eating at McDonalds is that you can always look forward to the same predictable menu of wholesome items almost anywhere in the world. That's how they've managed to stay on top—while feeding adults and kids of all ages a bland diet of greasy ground beef, laying lifelessly in between two dry buns. We all love their food.

Never to get left in the dust by their competitors, McDonalds has constantly tried out new taste sensations on their customers—often with limited success. But, you might ask, "What could the imaginative chefs at McDonalds possibly come up with that wouldn't be an instant hit?" Ahh, you'll see.

The Gurakoro

Out of the Japanese market's clamoring for something special came the Gurakoro—a hot sandwich made with deep fried macaroni, shrimp and mashed potatoes all nestled on a bed of cold cabbage. Yum yum. The McDonalds executives touted it as "Nothing like anything you've ever eaten before." And it wasn't. At least not all at the same time. Despite some marginal nutritional value, the Gurakoro failed miserably because it was just plain tasteless. Nevertheless, the Gurakoro still pops up at special times of the year, reminding Japanese customers that Quarter Pounders with Cheese aren't so bad after all.

The Hulaburger

After the Gurakoro fell on its face, Ray Krok (the owner and originator of McDonalds) came up with the idea for the Hulaburger. Created in 1963 to answer Roman Catholics' challenge of not being able to eat meat on Friday, the Hulaburger was basically a cheeseburger that replaced the meat with a thick slab of hot pineapple. It was an instant flop. Especially when the Catholics caught wind of an alternative product that tasted much better—the Filet-O-Fish sandwich.

The McDLT

Succumbing to customers' complaints about burgers with piping hot meat served with limpid lettuce and tomatoes, McDonalds came out with the McDLT. The McDLT was served to the customer in a special packaging tray—one side held the bottom bun, hot meat, cheese and sauces, while the other side held the cool lettuce, tomato, pickles and top half of the bun. When the consumer was handed the package, they had to "build it themselves"—a concept that did not go over well with lazy lunch goers. The packaging was unwieldy and over twice the size of the other burgers, so it filled up the back seat of their car in a hurry. Even after being rebranded as the Big N' Tasty, the public couldn't be fooled. The McDLT experienced a short life and died in the late 1980s.

The McLobster

For the more sophisticated diner, McDonalds came up with the McLobster sandwich. The McLobster was basically a hot dog bun filled with lobster and McDonald's secret sauce that looked suspiciously like vomit. And at $5.99, the McLobster was no Mcdeal. While you can still get your hands on a McLobster in some Canadian and Maine franchises, you might be better off to save your money and drive to a restaurant where you don't have to eat your seafood in the car.

The McHotDog

McDonalds CEO Ray Kroc was dead set against ever selling hot dogs at McDonalds. And, in fact, it wasn't until after his death, that selected McDonalds franchises in the Midwest opted to sell McHotDogs as popular summer items. Later, UK franchises sold them on their PoundSaver Menu, as did franchises at the Toronto Metro Zoo and the SkyDome. Tokyo stores attempted to revive the McHotDog several times—as late as 2009—but just couldn't make the item stick on their permanent menu.

McPizza

Pizza is big business. And McDonalds was aware of it, so in the mid 1990s, they decided to offer a bland imitation of pizza that people could buy elsewhere. After investing in expensive pizza ovens and widening the drive-thru windows, the McPizza ultimately came to an unseemly demise. Even though McDonalds customers appreciated fast food, they still had time to drive out of the way to their favorite pizza parlor.

McPasta

Another unpopular McDonalds menu item was McPasta. After rigorous testing in the southern United States and in Rochester, New York, McDonalds began offering lasagna, fettuccine alfredo and spaghetti with meatballs. Side dishes included mashed potatoes and gravy and boiled vegetables. Ultimately, McPasta met with the same demise as McPizza—fast food lovers who have come to identify McDonalds with cheeseburgers and fries just couldn't get their arms around pasta and mashed potatoes.

The McAfrica

About the time widespread African famine was plastered across the news, McDonalds decided to introduce their newest product—the McAfrica. Despite brilliant marketing, McDonalds felt bad about people chowing down into McAfricas while watching children starve on TV—even while providing donation boxes for famine relief.

The McLean Deluxe

By far, the biggest loser in the McDonalds lineup has to be the McLean Deluxe hamburger. It wasn't popular with women and men were turned off from the wimpy hamburger, served with a diet Coke. But the biggest reason why the McLean Deluxe failed was due to taste—it had none. In order to shave calories off of the burger, fat was extracted and replaced with water. And, to make the water stay put in the meat, it had to be mixed with carrageenan—seaweed. So, in the end, the new McDonalds product aimed at the calorie conscious tasted bad and didn't sell.

You'd think after that kind of track record, the big Chefs at McDonalds would stick to the things that work. But, bless their hearts, they keep on trying. Walk into any American McDonalds and you'll still find the Big N' Tasty, right along side the McRib, Chicken McNuggets, Sausage McGriddles and McFlurries with Oreo Cookies. Long live American ingenuity!

Watching Grandma Circle the Drain

There's only so many ways you can get rid of a dead body. Regardless of how it got that way—stabbed, shot, bludgeoned, run over by a truck, pummeled, poisoned, choked, tossed off a building or just withered from old age—its final demise has to be handled with care.

Up until recently, you only had two choices. You could bury Grandma in a casket or cremate her. Both cost a lot of money and take weeks of planning. Or, if money's tight, you could always drive into the middle of the desert in the dead of night, dig a hole by the glow of your car's headlights and toss Grammy in—sort of the Home Depot approach to traditional funeral services. It's done all the time—at least in gangster movies.

According to the National Funeral Directors Association, funerals can cost between $6,500 and $10,000. Cremations can be significantly cheaper, at $800. But then, there's that nagging question of what to do with those messy ashes. Do I keep them in an urn on top of the mantel or do I put them in a box out in the shed? And, who gets to keep them? What if I lose them?

Sixteen years ago, scientists came up with an alternative way to deal with human remains after a person's passing. The process is called alkaline hydrolysis and involves sprinkling the body with a highly alkaline product, such as lye, then subjecting the corpse to high temperatures and pressure in a specially designed cooker. After several hours of bubbling and gurgling, Grammy is reduced to the consistency of motor oil, with a few bone chips thrown in. Because the liquid is sterile, it can be safely poured down the drain, into the gutter or sprayed over your lawn. For the sentimental, the hydrolysis engineers can capture dried bones and other residue and store them in an urn, or a small container worn around your neck. That way, Grammy will never be too far away—even after she's gone.

While the process of alkaline hydrolysis may seem like a morbid way to end a loved one's life, it's been around for years—it's the gangster's first choice for eliminating snitches, backstabbers and turncoats because it's so easy. Just dump Larry the Lump into an empty ditch and cover him with lye. Over time, Larry's body decomposes without the dangerous emissions of carbon dioxide, toxic chemicals—or fingerprints.

Even though it's been around for quite some time, alkaline hydrolysis is usually a tough sell to grieving families. There's just something uncomfortable about saying good-bye to Grandma as she circles the drain. The other problem is that alkaline hydrolysis is only legal in two states: Minnesota and New Hampshire. Other states, including Ohio, California, Florida, Maine and Oregon have legislation pending. So, if hydrolysis appeals to you, you'll have to be sure that you include in your last will and testament, instructions for someone to drive you over the border. There are strict rules about transporting fruit, firearms and dead bodies across state lines, so you might want to check with authorities first—or stash the body in the trunk under the spare tire.

Despite its simplicity, the Roman Catholic Church has yet to climb on board the bandwagon. Patrick McGee, the spokesperson for the Roman Catholic Church Diocese of Manchester, NH states, "We believe this process which enables a portion of human remains to be flushed down a drain, to be undignified." But, George Carlson, the Industrial Waste Manager of the New Hampshire Department of Environmental Services defends hydrolysis by saying, "Things the public might find more troubling routinely flow into sewage treatment plants in the U.S. all the time. That includes blood and spillover embalming fluid from funeral homes."

When it comes to supporting alkaline hydrolysis for disposing of human remains, no one is more vocal than Brad Cain, President of BioSafe Engineering. BioSafe is the company that manufactures the unique steel containers used in alkaline hydrolysis and estimates that over 50 companies, including veterinary schools, pharmaceutical companies, universities and the United States Government are already using his products to dispose of animal carcasses, medical cadavers and other forms of human waste.

If time is running out for you or your loved ones and you're interested in using alkaline hydrolysis as the final goodbye, you may have to plan a bit. At the current time, there are only two facilities in the United States that will take Grandma in: the University of Florida in Gainesville and the Mayo Clinic in Rochester, Minnesota. Both offer their research facilities to the public and business is booming. People are just dying to get in.

Fun with Telemarketers

Several years ago, I met a lady through an online dating service and thought she could be "the one." Just to be safe, I bought a hefty supply of male enhancement drugs from an online Canadian pharmacy—just in case I needed them. I had no suspicions that I would, but it's like loading a gun—the best time to do it is before the action starts, not after. After receiving my first order, I was quite proud of myself for being so prepared and saving all that money—until I found out that I just sold my soul to the devil.

Most online Canadian pharmacies are actually located somewhere in the East—not near the changing leaves of Vermont or New Hampshire, but closer to the shifting sands of Bangalore, India. When you speak to a friendly sales rep named Mike or Richard, you're really talking to Maandhata or Radhakrishna who are eager to help you with your order. And your next. And your next.

As soon as I placed my first order from the online pharmacy, I found myself joined at their hips. On the bright side, I'll never have to be concerned with forgetting to refill my orders—Maandhata or Radhakrishna will be right there to remind me—at 2:00 in the morning, on holiday weekends, when I'm just about to sit down to Easter dinner or when I'm lying in Intensive Care. Come rain or come shine, Maandhata or Radhakrishna will never forget me. In fact, I can expect to hear from them at least three times a day, never taking 'no' for an answer. Finally, I had enough and asked Maandhata and Radhakrishna to please stop calling. They called bright and early the next morning.

Online pharmacies use all of the usual tricks of the trade with the tenacity of a barracuda. Once they get their teeth into you, it's easier just to cut off your arm than it is to look for a doctor. The Federal Communications

90

Commission suggests effective measures like asking to be placed on a "Do not call" list. You can also register all of your telephone numbers under your local provider's do not call registry, which makes it a fineable offense if they continue to bother you. None of that matters to Maandhata or Radhakrishna. You're in the United States. They're in India.

So, after Maandhata or Radhakrishna refused to stop calling me, I decided to take off the gloves and start playing dirty.

The first thing I tried was patiently listening to their entire sales pitch. When they were finished, I asked them what they were doing this weekend, were they single and did they have a girlfriend? Informing them that I was gay, I asked Maandhata and Radhakrishna if they would they like to fly over here and spend the weekend with me. Who knows? Maybe we could get married and they could give all of this up.

When I was lucky enough to get a call from Padma, I immediately lapsed into my Lithuanian with a Tagalog dialect. That's had some of the best results for deflecting unwanted sales calls. If that fails, I'll wait until she's finished her entire script covering this week's specials, then ask her what color underwear she's wearing. Click.

As things escalated, I started to fill them in on all of the ways I planned to relocate their first born male child. That worked for a while until I started getting calls from Aachman, Chaaruchandra, Egaiarasu, Gajananvihari, Ibraheem, Kailashchandra, Nabhanyu, Padmanabha, Radhana, Taanusiya, Vaijayantimala, Yaamoli and Phil.

A week later, Pachaimuthu called just to let me know that the Online Pharmacy was featuring a special on Dilantin and Topamax. I confessed to him that while I wasn't experiencing any grade II convulsions at the time, I'd sure appreciate it if he could help me out with some Demerol, Vicodin, Percocet or Oxycontin—pharmaceutical grade cocaine, heroin or medical marijuana if they have it. Click.

Another effective way to deal with online pharmacies is to revive some of your old college tricks. The next time Radhana, Taanusiya or Vaijayantimala call, try saying, "Oh, I'm so glad you called back. There's been a huge mistake in the order I just placed. Instead of two medium mushroom pizzas, I'd like an extra-large Meat-lover's Supreme with an order of hot wings and 2 liters of Coke. Can you help me with that?"

Many telemarketers are willing to work with you as long as you're willing to place an order. Since they only make $2.74 an hour, plus commission, they'll stay on the phone forever if you ask them to wait: "Just hold on for a moment while I go get my credit card." Then, grab your gym bag and run out the door to keep your racquetball appointment.

Another great way to take advantage of the silence is to involve the family by asking Radhana to, "Hold on for a moment while I get my last invoice." Then put the phone down in the middle of the dinner table with the speakerphone turned on. Speak loudly and ask your kids to pass the mashed potatoes, beans and chicken. Ask about what the kids did in school today and how soccer practice went. The goal is to see how long you can keep Radhana on the phone, wasting her valuable time. Buy ice cream for the person who keeps Radhana on the phone the longest—without a sale.

If you're not feeling particularly creative, there are some simple tricks you can use that are taught in the defensive portion of telemarketing school. First, tell them that you're a little busy at the moment, but please call me later at my mother's house. Then give them your supervisor's home phone number. If that doesn't work, ask them to please speak up—no matter how loudly they're speaking. The goal is to have them yelling into their headset. Or, you can ask them to repeat everything they say—as many times as they'll go for before hanging up. "What was that?" "Could you repeat that?" "I'm sorry, will you say that again?" Making telemarketers repeat everything five or six times will cut their sales performance down to nothing and get them in trouble with their supervisors, so they'll probably stop calling you. At least for a day or so.

Like all other low-paying jobs, telemarketers are only human and are in the business to make money, so if you're feeling empathetic, give them a break. The next time that Kailashchandra calls and asks you how you are, be honest. Tell her about everything that's ailing you this morning—start at the top of your head and work your way down to your feet. "Well,

I'm doing pretty well, except for my alcoholic hepatitis, anthrax, bacterial meningitis, bubonic plague, chronic fatigue syndrome, cretinism, diabetes, ebola, herpes, Huntington's disease, interstitial cystitis, jaundice, kwashiorkor, lead poisoning, malaria, Marburg fever, non-gonococcal urethritis, osteoporosis, polio, Rift Valley fever, SARS, shingles, typhoid, uremia, Von Hippel-Lindau disease and yellow fever. But, thank God the genital warts have gone away!"

Another effective approach involves getting the telemarketer interested in your business. Tell them you'll place an order with them, if they'll place an order for a case of your new Hawaiian print adult diapers. Explain that they'll be entered into a free drawing—first prize is a two week stay at the Hotel Stay Inn in Bangalore, India.

A tried and true method to get telemarketers to stop calling is by giving them a long list of all of your expired credit cards. Be patient. You're going to have to read them 12 to 14 sets of bogus numbers and wait until each one fails. After it's all over, ask them if you can send them an envelope containing change.

If all of these techniques fail, you're ready to pull out the big guns. First, tell them that the person they're trying to contact has just passed away. It had something to do with the drugs they purchased from you, so you should be hearing from their lawyer next week. Or, tell them that the FBI has a wiretap on your phone because your little brother was kidnapped last night. But feel free to call back anytime.

By this time, most telemarketers will get the message, the only other options you have left are the easiest—and the ones you probably should have tried first. Go to www.donotcall.gov and register your telephones against telemarketers. If that doesn't work, try asking the telemarketer not to call. Who knows? It just might work.

Intercourse and Horneytown

Whether you live in a small town or a large city, where you ultimately plant your feet has a lot to say about who you are. Some people choose to live in places like Wetwang, England because they work there. Others have deep rooted family trees in Looneyville, Minnesota. And what high-powered executive wouldn't jump at the chance to get transferred to Goosepimple Junction, Virginia? To help you decide where to make your next move, here are a few places you won't want to miss investigating:

Intercourse, Pennsylvania—With its unusually suggestive name, it's hard for most people to believe that Intercourse, PA is located in the heart of Amish country. In fact, it was the location of the blockbuster movie, "Witness" starring Harrison Ford. Prior to 1814, it was named Cross Keys because two major highways intersected at its location. In the early days of the village, the word intercourse was commonly used to mean fellowship or social interaction.

Wide Awake, Colorado—One night when a group of miners were sitting around a campfire, they were trying to come up with a good name for their new town. After passing a bottle around late into the night, someone finally said, "Let's just turn in and talk about it more when we're wide awake." "That's it!" shouted one of the miners. "Let's call it Wide Awake!"

Peculiar, Missouri—Thirty miles south of Kansas City laid a small community needing a name. In the early days, the town never really needed one, so the town folk put off naming their community until getting their first post office required one. The postmaster wrote the United States Government asking for the name "Excelsior." The name was already taken. He wrote for permission to use another and another until he was so exasperated that he told them, "We'll take any name you have available as long as it's peculiar."

Toad Suck, Arkansas—Before the Army Corps of Engineers completed a highway bridge over the Arkansas River in 1973, the most reliable way to get from one side of the river to the other was by barge. Next to the river stood an old tavern where many of the bargemen would pull over to drink rum and moonshine. There, they would "suck on bottles until they swelled up like toads"—hence one version of how the town got its name.

Pee Pee Township, Ohio—Surprisingly, Pee Pee Township gets its name from nearby Pee Pee Creek (actually, it's P.P. Creek) that took its name from an Irish Settler in 1798 and not because people urinate there. It is one of 14 townships in Pike County, Ohio and boasted more than 7,000 residents in the 2000 census.

Accident, Maryland—The town of Accident traces its history back to 1750 when a local resident named George Deakins accepted 600 acres from King George II of England in relief of a debt. George sent out two independent surveying parties to find the best 600 acres in the county—neither of which was aware of the other. By coincidence, they both surveyed the same plot, beginning at the same tree. Confident that no one else owned the property, Mr. Deakins named the tract the "Accident Tract"—on purpose.

Hell, Michigan—There are several theories as to how Hell, Michigan got its name. One theory suggests that two traveling Germans stepped out of a stagecoach and remarked, "So schön und hell!" which loosely translates to "So beautiful and bright!" Hearing this, the neighbors focused on the latter part of the statement. Another theory is that one of the early settlers named George Reeves (not the actor who played Superman) was asked what they should call the town. Always the eloquent gentleman, Reeves replied, "For all I care, you can name it Hell!"

Horneytown, North Carolina—Located in Forsythe County, just east of Winston-Salem, Horneytown gets its name from early pioneers. Not pioneers with rampant sex drives, but rather the Horney family who had established farming and a flourishing business community before the Civil War.

Saint-Louis-du-Ha! Ha!, Quebec—Saint-Louis-du-Ha! Ha! is a small parish located near the south shore of the Saint Lawrence River. Its name refers to nearby Lake Temiscouata and is one of the few towns in the world that legally contains exclamation points in its name. Ha Ha is an archaic French term for an unexpected obstacle or abruptly ending path.

Ding Dong, Texas—Despite evidence to the contrary, the town of Ding Dong, Texas was not named after Peter Hansborough Bell, the third Governor of Texas. Nor was it named for the Hostess snack cake or because it's located in Bell County. Back in the 1930s, brothers Zulis and Bert Bell owned a country store and hired a creative sign painter named C.C. Hoover to put up a new sign. Hoover suggested that he dress up the sign by painting two bells on the sign with the words, "Ding Dong." The surrounding community quickly took to the name.

Tightwad, Missouri—During the town's early days, a local store owner cheated a customer (who just happened to be a postman) by charging him an extra 50 cents for a watermelon. To get back at the proprietor, the postman started delivering mail to the new town of Tightwad, Missouri.

The Real Secret to Using On-line Dating

It's Saturday night around 11:30 and I've been telling Carol about the time I visited Nepal while on break from Harvard Medical School. I was telling Leslie how much I excel at skiing the steeps in the Chugach mountain range and Sharon and I were engaged in a long discussion about our favorite restaurants in Tuscany. All from the comfort of my living room.

I haven't been on a date in over five years; ever since my wife left me for the Bowflex repairman. So, it's easy to understand why I've so grown comfortable with sidling up to women through Match.com, Great-Expectations.com, OverThirtySingles.com, True.com and Plentyof Fish.com—while wallowing in the safety that only deception and miles of distance can provide. But recently, I've started to grow suspicious of the women I've been meeting after reading their on-line profiles. They all seem to sound suspiciously the same.

So, after more than 45 minutes of exhaustive research, I came up with an interpretive approach for anyone hoping to find "Mr. or Ms. Right" over their wireless network.

Your first step when touring on-line dating sites should be to throw out any precept of honesty; this is hardcore self—aggrandizement at its finest. This is obviously not for people watching their sodium intake. You have to take everything you read with a grain of salt. Make that a salt mine.

Avoid anyone who goes by fascinating login names like "MountainGirl," "MrFit," "SexyBlonde," "WorldTraveler," "Love2Ski" or "Luv2HaveFun." These are handles of people who live in the slums, spend all day on the couch and haven't laughed since the Nixon administration.

Be careful of the pictures that people post. No one, no matter who they are, is going to use any photo of them that's less than 10 years old. Dead giveaways of bogus photos are suspicious backgrounds like the first flight at Kitty Hawk or the Korean War. You'll never see any photos that show what the person is really about, either. If people were really truthful with their on-line profiles, instead of posting snapshots of themselves dancing the night away on a cruise ship in the Bahamas, they'd post photos of themselves scratching their butt in a pair of stained underwear, while dragging around a half-eaten bag of Doritos.

About Me

Now we come to the section called, "About Me . . ." The About Me section is meant to briefly sum up your love interest's likes, dislikes and accomplishments. The problem is, everyone lies. No one is going to admit that they've been working in the same windowless cubicle for over 25 years and still lives with their parents. So, to help get to the truth, I've compiled a handy translation guide to interpret what your web mate is saying and what they really mean:

What the profiles say	What they really mean
▪ I am fun and energetic.	▪ I'm immature and can't focus on anything for more than 3 minutes.
▪ I have a great sense of humor and love to laugh.	▪ When I'm taking my anti-depressants, I can find simple ways to amuse myself.
▪ I enjoy skiing, hiking, walking my dog, buttered popcorn at the movies, renting DVDs, listening to live music, dancing and reality TV.	▪ I like getting drunk at bars in ski lodges, picking up the poop that my mutt has left behind, stuffing my face with junk food, vegging out with DVD rentals, taking my clothes off at sleazy piano bars and laying comatose in front of just about anything that's on TV.
▪ I've been around the block.	▪ I'm tired, old and my skin hangs off just about every part of my body.

- I enjoy good food and wine. ▶ - I wouldn't know gourmet food if you threw it at me and I've never drank from a bottle that didn't have a screw top.

- At this time, I am self-employed. ▶ - Nobody can stand to work with me.

- I'm not into money. ▶ - I haven't had anything in my bank account since my Bar Mitzvah.

- I am someone that likes adventure and having fun but also loves being home. ▶ - My idea of a good time is dodging bill collectors and peeking out of my bedroom window to make sure they don't repossess my car.

- I'm very active and always into new challenges and living life to its fullest. ▶ - I'm a neurotic, agitated loser who's always looking for a scam or a shortcut to riches.

- I am not your typical mate. ▶ - I've never gotten past a first date. Ever.

- I have an entertaining personality. ▶ - I have a lot of undiagnosed nervous ticks, twitches and mannerisms.

- In my spare time, I enjoy being with my family and friends. ▶ - I live at home with my parents, three aunts, their eight step children and 10 cats. They're the only ones who will have me.

- I am a true romantic who is waiting to meet the person of their dreams. ▶ - I'm a dreamer who spends all of their spare time surfing porn sites.

- My mother is Dutch and my biological father is from Mexico. ▶ - My mother was a hooker from Amsterdam who was knocked up by a merchant marine while on shore leave in Tijuana.

The Search . . .

The logical starting point for finding your mate is to make your search criteria as similar to yourself as you can. Most on-line daters start with a search radius of 20 or 30 miles within their own zip code. For compatibility sake, they'll shoot for an age spread of 5 to 10 years on either side of their own age and throw in a few sizzling keywords like "hot," "sexy" or "athletic" just for good measure. I've never had any luck with this type of approach. Instead, I'll throw the net out a little wider and include all women between the ages of 15 and 85, locales that include Afghanistan, the Far East and the more remote parts of the Ukraine.

Once you finally find a few unsuspecting victims to snag, most dating services have a number of anonymous methods of contacting your prospects. The first is the wink. A wink is a safe way of showing someone you're interested without suffering any embarrassing repercussions—sort of like tossing a dead tuna off the stern to see if you can lure a shark into the boat.

The second tool at your disposal is the anonymous email. Since most on-line dating services routinely filter emails between clients, you're not allowed to send them your real email address. Instead, every now and again, you'll get a nice little note in your inbox that says something like, "You've got a new message from Blonde4U; Subject: Leave Me Alone or I'll Get a Restraining Order!"

About My Life . . .

If you're not turned off by now, you've got one more, handy tool to use: the "About My Life" summary. If you were to reduce your entire life into a single paragraph, it would look something like this:

Hair: Lots of it growing on my back
Eyes: Bloodshot
Best feature: Love handles
Body art: Tons of tattoos

Sports and exercise: Mutton busting, throwing rocks at cars, arm wrestling, tossing the boomerang, spraying graffiti on underpasses, log rolling, jousting, tug of war, holding my breath
Exercise habits: Only out of necessity
Daily diet: Anything that I don't have to make myself
Interests: Smoking cigarettes, recreational drug use, tattoos, body piercing, burglary, discovering new porn sites
Education: Left school after the 3rd grade
Occupation: Unemployed
Income: An allowance from my mother
Languages: Some English, Tagalog, fluent Yiddish
Sign: Stop
My place: Or yours?
Pets I have: Pythons (12)
Pets I like: Various reptiles, fleas, maggots, gerbils, pit bulls

So, you see, there's no excuse to be alone these days. Not as long as you have a computer. So fire up your PC, stretch out in front of a roaring fire with a can of beer and your keyboard and get ready to meet Mr. or Ms. Right! They're out there waiting for you.

Coming In for a Landing

Of the millions of absurd inventions advertised on TV, only a few have piqued my interest enough to lighten my wallet. There have been thousands of ingenious tools meant to make life easier that didn't appeal to me in the least—anything having to do with golf, children, pets, boating, bowling, women's products (although I confess to trying out the butt lifter for two weeks before returning it), any form of tool associated with hunting wild animals or washing cars. Some inventions haven't progressed much further than the patent stage. That doesn't mean that they weren't good ideas. They just need a little more time to gather a following. Others could be on the brink of changing my life.

One of the problems I've wrestled with my entire life is knowing when I'm going to die. Entering appointments into my Blackberry and remembering holidays gives me a reason to live. On the other hand, not knowing exactly when I'm going to depart this earth is not only frustrating, it causes a lot of problems and costs me money. If I knew that I was going to have a fatal heart attack tomorrow morning, I wouldn't worry about eating a double bacon cheeseburger for dinner or paying next month's mortgage. If I was absolutely sure that I had only hours to live, I'd put it into overdrive and buy that $500 million life insurance policy for my family.

So, as a mere mortal, I was ecstatic to learn that someone has already patented a tool that can help me pin-point with accuracy, just when I'm going to go. It's called the Life Expectancy Watch.

The **Life Expectancy Watch** is a handy timepiece that you wear on your arm, just like a wristwatch. But, instead of keeping track of time as it marches forward, it lets you know how much time you have left on earth. When you open the box, the first thing you notice is that time is already running out. Don't let that bother you. Before it will tell you exactly when you're going to keel over, you have to calibrate it according to the enclosed actuarial table that lists variables like your age, gender, where you live, who you associate with, if you smoke or drink, how many outstanding arrest warrants you have and other things that will impact your lifespan. A 57-year-old, alcoholic bank robber riding with the Oakland Hells Angels is likely to have worse news ahead of him than a 27-year-old, yoga instructor living in Maui.

The face of the watch displays large, easy to read numbers, indicating the time you have left on earth in years, months, days and minutes. What could be better? It also has an illuminated face, so you can read it at night AND it's waterproof, so you can wear it surfing in Hawaii or floating face down in the Hudson River.

The Life Expectancy Watch comes with a number of handy buttons that will help you fine-tune your mortal end. For instance: I don't like to skydive, but if I did, buttons on the face of the watch would allow me to tick off valuable minutes from my life—even if I survived a crash. And, if you love foods ladened with fat and cholesterol, you can easily shorten your life by the push of a button. It even has helpful acceleration and deceleration settings that will make the watch run faster during the Christmas holidays when you're pounding down the egg nog and smoking cigars and slower when you're spending the weekend at your in-laws. And, if you're one of those people who need to be reminded about everything, you can set the alarm to inform you of your last minutes on earth.

The **Meditation Bag** is a useful tool for people who just can't find a quiet place to get away for 20 minutes. Made from the same space age fabric used by astronauts, the Meditation Bag is large enough to completely encompass an average adult, leaving plenty of room for an iPod, meditation mat and other essential accessories. All you have to do is find an empty closet, garage, rooftop or flat spot on the edge of a cliff and climb in. The Meditation Bag zips up the front, leaving a small area that surrounds the nose and mouth—just enough to breathe.

The Meditation Bag is perfect for short trips to nirvana, or long spiritual weekends. It could easily be enhanced with incense holders and battery-operated exhaust fans to help control the inside temperature. If you enjoy meditating out in the winter wilderness, a goose down liner would help keep you warm and toasty. By attaching external bags for food, trash and urine containers, you'd be good to go for days at a time.

Even with everything the Meditation Bag has to offer, sometimes it's still hard to find time when your family will leave you alone. That's why the Meditation Bag would come in a variety of camouflage patterns and colors. You could choose from favorites like piles of old soiled laundry, dirty oily rags, leaves or dirt—things you know your family will never go near. The Meditation Bag would come with a breathing tube, should you wish to be buried in the backyard. Just be sure to mail the enclosed Police Retrieval Form, letting the authorities know when to come and dig you up. Ahhh . . . peace and serenity has never been easier.

Whether I'm running from the police, trying to catch a bus or taking my first ski run at Vail, there's something else I can also count on running—my nose. And who hasn't walked up to a friend on a brisk winter morning with a two-inch booger hanging from the tip of their beak? That's why I was so happy to hear about the **Nose Wipe**. The Nose Wipe is a refillable container that you wear around your wrist, like a wrist watch. Filled with absorbent material, the Nose Wipe lets you swipe your index finger across your nose, then wipe it off inside the Nose Wipe instead of on the outside of your sleeve or on someone's back.

Secured with a wide elastic band, the Nose Wipe can take a beating—like being mugged on a subway, a tough game of rugby or having sex in the utility closet with the maid. Each order comes with six Nose Wipe refills and a convenient re-order form. And for those with sensitive noses, you could order refills that are hypo-allergenic and coated with aloe vera. As the manufacturer says, "The Nose Wipe is Snot a Bad Idea!"

As I get older, there's one thing that seems to increase besides my age: the number of nighttime visits to the toilet. There's no getting around it, blindly fumbling my way from the dark bedside, down the hall to the commode can be risky business, resulting in stubbed toes and broken furniture. One alternative is to turn on the lights, blinding the entire family. Thankfully, there is another way.

Toilet Landing Lights were developed for people who are tired of whacking their knees while shuffling through dark rooms to find the bathroom. Toilet Landing Lights use proven aviation technology, creating a circle of gentle blue lights that are mounted under the rim of the urinal, emitting a gentle glow—much like coming in for a landing on an airplane. It takes less than 15 minutes to attach the lights to the commode. They even come with their own portable battery pack, so you can take them with you when you spend the weekend at relatives'.

When visiting the can in the dark, not only will you know where the commode is, you'll be able to tell whether or not someone's left the lid down, preventing you from peeing all over the walls and the floor. And if you have limited visibility leading to the downstairs bathroom, you'll want to opt for the additional "Runway Light Kit"—two strips of friendly white lights that point you safely to the entrance to the bathroom—just like an airstrip.

Toilet Landing Lights can be ordered singly, in pairs, in a variety of attractive colors and with pulsating bulbs to give you that real airport runway feeling. The only thing missing is the flight attendant instructing you to return to your seat!

It's hard to imagine that these inventions haven't taken off and flooded the markets by now. Just like the Alarm Fork, Big Balls, Beerella, Diaper Alarm, Fingertip Toothbrush, Kissing Shield, Kneepad Earmuffs and the Wearable Dog House, they probably just need a little more time. Most good products do.

My Birth Anomalies

Anita Phillips was ugly. I should know. I had to sit behind her, looking at the back of her head during the entire sixth grade. She had big ears, stringy hair and bumps on her head the size of golf balls. If her parents weren't so cheap, they would have sought the services of a good plastic surgeon for her and spared me a lifetime of suffering. But things could have been worse. In between looking at the back of Anita's head and staring off into space, I tried to imagine what it would be like to have birth anomalies more serious than big ears. Like having two left feet.

As I imagine it, having two left feet could present just as many advantages as disadvantages. True, having two left feet would put me into a perpetual right-hand turn, but I'd never have to worry if I had my shoes on the correct feet when I got dressed in the dark. And, although there would always be a tendency for my body to list toward the right, I could easily compensate for it by assuming a super-wide stance. I could buy dozens of pairs of shoes and give all the "righties" to some needy person who was oppositely afflicted.

Another anomaly I wouldn't mind having is "eyes in the back of my head." Having both eyes looking forward is supposed to be one of man's greatest advantages over the other species. With both eyes in front, we're supposed to have better depth perception and improved peripheral vision. But, I've always found that having both eyes in front of my head has made it a lot easier for class clowns to tape "kick me" signs on my back.

Having eyes in the back of my head could help me assess the past and make decisions on how I might have done things better. When one of my friends asked me, "Did you see the rack on that chick?" I'd just answer, "Yeah. I'm looking at them now." Having eyes in the back of my head could potentially eliminate thousands of moving violations over the years—most importantly, speeding tickets. Of course, there could also be some disadvantages. Getting a haircut could be tricky. The first thing I'd have to do is remind my hair stylist, "Hey, just to let you know . . . I have a couple of eyes to watch out for back there." Not only would it keep her on her toes, there'd be no need for the hand mirror inspection when she was done.

With eyes in the back of my head, I'd have to change my entire approach to walking, running, skiing and swimming. Swimming would be much more enjoyable. Since my eyes would be facing up, I could gaze up at the sky while doing laps and I'd save money by eliminating goggles. Adapting to walking could be tough. It would mean that I'd either have to be constantly looking over my shoulder or contrive some sort of mirrored contraption to wear around my neck—like bicyclists use to see behind them.

I've also thought it would be great to have "eyes bigger than my stomach." Now, that could mean one of two things: either I had a tiny, little stomach that would need to be constantly fed, or I would have two huge eyes. Since the average human stomach is about 12 inches long, I'd have to have a face the size of a washing machine to accommodate eyes that big. Assuming that my eyes were that large, I'd be able to take in enormous amounts of visual stimuli. My contact lenses would be the size of Frisbees and would require both hands just to remove them. While I'd never have to worry about losing one in the carpet, it would cost me a fortune in wetting solution.

I can also see the value in "being all thumbs." Having opposing thumbs is what is supposed to set man apart from the rest of the animal kingdom, but it's not always what it's cracked up to be. Take hitchhiking. Currently, hitchhikers only have two positions—forehand and backhand. Hitchhikers with 10 thumbs would have an infinite variety of stances—handy for spending long hours on the road. On the flip side, being all thumbs could present a number of challenges. I've never had much success picking my nose with my thumb. And, imagine how difficult it would be to perform brain surgery with 10 thumbs. On the other hand, if I were a criminal it would be nearly impossible to identify me from a set of 10 identical thumbprints.

I'd like to have a "grin from ear to ear." There could be a lot of advantages to having a mouth that hinged near my ears, letting me split my head down the middle into two sections. Cleaning my teeth would be a snap for my dental hygienist. I could just lay my head back, open it in half and relax. Of course, since my mouth would be so much wider, I'd probably have 20 or 30 extra teeth, so it would cost more. My approach to shaving would have to change. And unless my date had the same anomaly, that first alarming kiss would look like an attack from Jaws.

If I had my way, I'd also like to be "all ears." If I were all ears, I might have a head covered with pinnas and ear canals, leaving little room for eyes or a nose—which would be OK if I had eyes in the back of my head. And, it begs the question, how would all of those ears be distributed? Would they flower concentrically around a logical center on my forehead, or would they be layered like a shingled roof? Who's to say that they wouldn't completely cover my body?

If I had ears completely covering my body, it would be much easier to listen into other people's conversations. If I needed someone to repeat something, instead of leaning my head toward them, I could just reach out my hand. On the downside, being all ears would mean I'd have to budget for thousands of Q-tips a month—to keep up with the never-ending build-up of wax.

In addition to anomalies with body parts, there would also be dozens of colors I could assimilate: "green with envy," "tickled pink," and "white as a sheet" to name a few. If I were really capable of becoming green with envy, I'd probably get invited to a lot more Christmas and St. Patrick Day parties—although it would severely restrict my fashion choices. If I were ever sick with jaundice, my skin would turn blue instead of yellow.

If I were "tickled pink," people would constantly mistake me for being sunburned and slather me SPF300. On the plus side, they'd never be able to tell if I was embarrassed, so I'd be free to fart in the elevator.

If I were "white as a sheet," I'd never be able to tan and I'd constantly get lost in between my sheets.

Beyond all of these physical anomalies, there are a host of others that I haven't had time to explore, like "being beside myself," "letting the cat get my tongue," "having a frog in my throat" or "putting my foot in my mouth." I'll save those for another day.

I'm Getting Old

The Merriam-Webster Dictionary defines the term old as "dating from the remote past," "persisting from an earlier time," "showing the effects of age," "no longer in use" and "used to express affection." That's me, alright—dating from the remote past and no longer in use. Although I am occasionally called upon to express affection

Thinking back over my life, the only time I used to ponder the passage of time was when I didn't have enough of it. Like the endless waiting until I was finally old enough to ride Space Mountain at Disneyland. I waited YEARS for my head to reach the bottom of that sign. The next time age became a factor was the l-o-n-g stretch between 18 and 21—I was old enough to enlist in the Navy and go halfway around the world, but still had to buy my beer out of the back of some guy's trunk in a vacant field. After reaching 21, the rest of my life became this vast, arid expanse, void of any notable milestones—until I reached 40.

Ask anyone (especially women) and they'll tell you that things really start to go to hell by the time you reach 40. At 40, I felt the immediate effects of gravity pulling me out to sea like a pacific tsunami. My metabolism was well on its way into its suicidal dive, meaning that I actually had to start counting calories. I could eat one plain rice cake and have to go out and buy bigger pants. Sure, exercise helped, but when you run one hour a day and sit or sleep for 23, the competition is fierce. My Fat Ass: 1—Me: 0

My greatest battle is avoiding the diagonal belt. For those of you unfamiliar with the diagonal belt, it's an old belt that is too small to completely surround the blubber you've accumulated around your waist while it struggles against the forces of gravity to remain parallel to the floor. So, the belt holds on for dear life in the small of your back, while the front slides down to a 45 degree angle, with your beer belly hanging over the top of it. The myth, of course, is that as long as I can continue wearing this belt, I'm not slipping as fast as I thought I was. I can brag to friends, "I still wear the same belt I wore in high school." Just at a different angle.

I've also had to learn how to avoid showing the world my "muffin top." A muffin top is similar to a 45 degree belt, except that it completely encircles your waist. The solution is to buy bigger and bigger pants and never tuck your shirt in. As long as you have something hiding your waist, no one ever has to know that you have a muffin top. It can be 115° while sitting outside by the pool in Desert Hot Springs and I'll always have a sweater tied around my waist—just in case it gets cool.

Relaxed fit jeans have helped. In fact, Americans have become so fat it's hard to find any other type. Relaxed fit jeans are made from an elastic material that "stretches with you as you move"—the manufacturers words, not mine. And, if relaxed fit jeans don't help, you can buy pants with adjustable elastic tabs on either side your waist. These handy little devices allow you to let the waist out on your pants as much as four inches without going back to Walmart for a larger pair.

Everything takes longer as I age. When I was 20, I could be dressed and out the bedroom window in 60 seconds—just as I heard my girlfriend's husband pull into their driveway. Now, I lie in bed each morning for over 20 minutes before swinging my feet around to the floor. Like an experienced airline pilot, I perform a pre-flight check of all my systems before rolling towards the runway. Then, it's the shuffle off to the bathroom.

I've noticed that most older people's bathrooms have one thing in common: they have huge medicine cabinets. Not big. Huge. They're necessary to contain all of the prescription and over the counter medicines we now require. I have one entire shelf devoted to prescription drugs, arranged by expiration date and the time of day they're supposed to be taken. I have over 30 bottles of prescription medicines that I haven't the foggiest idea why they were originally prescribed to me—but I don't dare throw them out. If I needed them once, chances are I'll need them again.

On the shelves below the prescriptions, I keep the necessary salves, balms, laxatives, sprays, lotions, eye drops, Advil, Fleets enema kits, Q-tips, Beano

111

caplets, allergy meds, patches (both hot and cold), rubs, pills, hemorrhoid creams, sleep aids, tubes, applicators, measuring cups and sponges that I need to get through the day.

Underneath the sink I keep a supply of contact lenses, solutions, glasses, extra reading glasses, braces, ace bandages, supports, electric toothbrushes, water piques, toothbrush sanitizers, plaque removers, blood pressure monitors, TMJ appliances, heating pads, ice packs, sleep apnea aids and support stockings that could compete with the inventory of a Costco pharmacy. And that's not including the drawer in my night stand reserved for sexual wellness helpers like Viagra, Cialis, Levitra, lubricants, jellies, condoms, pumps, male enhancement creams, contraceptives and heaven forbid, home pregnancy tests. Just in case.

One of the most puzzling things for me as I've aged has been the inevitable movement of hair from one location on my body to another. When I was young, hair grew on my head. It wasn't found anywhere else. As I matured into puberty, it began growing on my arms, legs and more private places. Things stayed pretty much that way for dozens of years. Once I hit 50, I noticed the slow migration of hair from my head as it headed south for the winter. The once smooth and silky skin on my shoulders and back has become densely forested with fields of thick, ape-like hair.

Perplexed by this unbridled phenomenon, I went to the Internet to try to learn why it should be so. The only thing that I've come up with is that as you age, hair covers sensitive parts of the body for extra warmth, protection and lubrication. I thought about this for a while, but I still haven't come up with any reasons why I now need more hair on the inside of my ears and nose and less hair on the top of my head. Nor can I come up with one good reason why my back needs to be any warmer at 50 than at 18.

Fifty years ago, I never wrote anything important enough to be shared with anyone—at least simultaneously. There were no photocopiers, fax machines or emails. If I wanted more than one person to read something I wrote, I'd have to hand deliver it to them or send it in an envelope via interoffice mail. Important documents were typed in triplicate—three sheets of typing paper, separated by carbon paper.

Today, it's much easier to share information. Most of the time, my words never get to experience the feel of being on paper. After blasting out my sentiments on why there is too much information bombarding people, I just send it to everyone on my mailing list using email, Facebook, Twitter, LinkIn, MyPage and snail mail. I don't even have to be in the office. I keep my laptop, iPad, Blackberry or iPhone with me at all times.

A few other developments remind me of how old I'm getting with each passing day. Arguably the most important invention has been the remote control that surfaced in 1955. When I was young, remote controls only did only one thing—they changed the channels on a television. Simply by pointing it in the general direction of the TV, you could miraculously switch between Adam 12 and The Dick Van Dyke Show without ever disturbing the permanent imprint of your heiney on the sofa.

Now, Universal Remote Controls manipulate everything in the house from my flatscreen television to the DVR, the microwave oven, my home computer, the thermostat on the hot tub, the temperature inside the wine cooler, my iPod, digital blender and double-wide refrigerator. It can even help me start my car if I need to make an early morning run to the Emergency Room because I haven't moved from the couch for the past three days.

In the same year that the remote control materialized, Raytheon invented the microwave oven (previously called the radar range) that has allowed me to completely eliminate cooking nutritious meals at home. In their place, I can zap popcorn, TV dinners or nachos in less time than it takes a commercial to run. Other time saving devices that I've experienced in my lifetime are cordless tools, my DirectTV satellite dish, LED flat panel screens, cell phones, ATMs, iPods, integrated circuit boards, Velcro, MRIs, coronary bypass surgery, GPSs, the personal computer, music synthesizers, smoke detectors, DNA fingerprinting, laser beams, superglue, digital music, waffle-soled running shoes and most important—Prozac. After all. I'm getting old.

New Rules for Deer and Elk Hunting Season!

It's late summer and in just a few short weeks, our national forests will once again be teeming with overweight, beer-guzzling, ATV thrashing, middle-aged men bonding with their offspring, engaged in an annual wilderness right of passage: deer and elk hunting season.

Across the United States, there have always been three traditional hunting seasons: archery, muzzleloader, followed by high-power rifle season. Short of running and hiding, deer and elk have stood absolutely defenseless against this barrage of artillery.

Forced to live off the land by just their instincts and lightning-fast reactions, wildlife are helpless against man-made weapons of mass destruction. So, to correct the problem, the US Fish and Wildlife Service and the Department of Agriculture has agreed to replace the three traditional hunting seasons with fairer, more humane seasons meant to "level the playing field" for deer and elk. They are wrestling season, primitive weapons season followed by knife fighting season.

Amateur and professional wrestling is the life-blood of all young men from high school age into young adulthood. So, it only makes sense that it should be integrated into the great American pastime: deer and elk hunting.

Wrestling season is designed to balance the contest between even the best hunters and the hunted. Playing by the rules of the wilderness, deer and elk stand to win at least an occasional contest against man. Instead of high-powered weapons, hunters will have to stalk and bring down their prey through a number of legal take down moves such as the Antler Smash,

Flying Arm Scissor, Jawbreaker, Hoof Drop, Reverse Neck Snap, Argentine Pile Driver, Body Slam, Full Nelson and Leg Scissor Takedown.

While it's true that few deer and elk are as yet schooled against these maneuvers, they can still flee into the brush until they've had time to take classes in the new techniques. Hunters participating in wrestling season will be required to wear traditional competitive wrestling shorts, boots, kneepads and headgear. There are no uniform requirements for the wildlife at this time.

Wrestling season will also create an entirely new cottage industry. Wilderness wrestling schools will start popping up all over the country, replacing obsolete gun shops and rifle ranges. Instead of relying on the cowardly skill of a clean shot from 75 yards, hunters will need to learn the importance of sneaking up on their prey and pinning them to the ground using a Full Nelson. Of course, with the new regulations will come the necessity for rule enforcement. Wilderness Umpires, employees of the USDA Forest Service, will prowl the outback, recording mat pins and resolving disputes between the hunter and the hunted.

If wilderness wrestling season catches on, you may even see other styles proliferate, such as Greco-Wilderness wrestling, Wilderness Judo wrestling, Brazilian Jiu-Jitsu Wilderness wrestling and of course, Wilderness Sumo wrestling.

During primitive weapons season, hunters will be restricted to using weapons whose origin was prior to the 17th century. These include spears, blowguns, rocks, sticks, morning stars, nail bats, punji sticks, torches, bolas, chakras, atlatls, meteor hammers, quarterstaffs, ballistas and slingshots. If the hunters so desire, they may also build elaborate forts, surrounded by moats and build catapults to subdue their prey with large boulders.

Primitive weapons season is aimed at bringing back the festive mood of the Middle Ages: when warriors sought deer and elk for food instead of trophies. And just to maintain the authentic flavor of the season, hunters will be required to wear full suits of armor, helmets with faceguards, breastplates, knight gauntlets and chain mail undergarments. Horses and

ATV's are prohibited during primitive weapons season; all hunts are to be conducted exclusively on foot.

What orphan, juvenile delinquent or young buck doesn't love a good knife fight? To help bring the wilderness experience to the masses, this year the Department of Wildlife has added the excitement of knife fighting to deer and elk hunting season.

During knife fighting season, hunters will be required to stalk their prey on foot, goading them into confrontations using a series of taunts and insults. Tactics include making defamatory remarks about the deer's mother, their ethnic heritage and who their doe has been sleeping with.

Any weapon with a blade is allowed. This includes axes, box cutters, daggers, rondels, long swords, pizza cutters, machetes and disposable razors. Knife fights may be conducted one-on-one or in gangs of hunters against bucks. A minimum of 3 participants on each side is required for a legal, gang-knife fight.

As a true aficionado of the wilderness experience, it's wonderful to know that this year man and wildlife will finally be on equal footing, just as they were so many years ago. So grab your spears and nunchuks; it's time to go hunting!

When Criminals Make a Mess

After losing my job two years ago, I needed cash and I wasn't above doing anything to get it—short of selling my blood, donating sperm, robbing a bank, picking up dog poop or greeting at Walmart. Then, a quote leapt out at me from an article in the L.A. Times about a high paying, alternative job that didn't require a college degree or years of specialized training. Simply put, it said:

"It's time to quit telling all of your friends, SOMEDAY I'm going to be a *Crime Scene Cleaner*. The time is TODAY."

Under even the best of circumstances, I imagined that cleaning up an urban crime scene would be a dirty job. Hours, days and sometimes weeks after a drug deal has gone bad, somebody has to come in and clean up the mess David Caruso has left behind. But, to clarify: as a crime scene cleaner, *you* won't be wearing an Armani suit while tiptoeing *your* way through the crime scene in *your* Berluti loafers. *You* won't be handing minute carpet fibers to your sexy lab assistant as she presses her cleavage into *your* face. *You* won't even get to carry a gun or drive a Hummer. What you will be doing is working long, hot hours in a sealed bio-decontamination suit while shoveling pounds of human tissue and brain matter off what was once an expensive bamboo floor. This is not the stuff you see on TV.

Crime scene decontamination companies (called CTS Decon crews) are big business in urban centers like Miami, Los Angeles, Chicago and New York. Smaller cities like Mayberry probably have them too, but Barney Fife, Sheriff Taylor and Aunt Bee are usually responsible for cleaning up Floyd the barber after he's blown his head off in the back of his barber shop.

Up until recently, there were relatively few companies that could return a blood-spattered crime scene to its fastidious, original condition. In 2008, there were only 300 companies, each handling over 400 cases a year, 24 hours a day, 7 days a week. Most Decon crews are contracted by local police departments and insurance companies to return the residences to their original condition, charging the home owners between $1,000 to $6,000.

In the case of Methamphetamine labs, the work is a little more complicated. Since everything capable of absorbing toxic chemicals like methanol, ammonia, benzene and hydrochloric acid must be removed and destroyed, usually all of the furniture, carpeting and internal sheet rock (and even the 2 x 4s that frame the wall) must be completely replaced before it can be restored to its original condition.

Even after reading all of this, my interest was still piqued (or should I say, I was still broke), so I looked into how much money I could make as a CTS decon crew member. After all, there has to be a catch somewhere, or else everyone would want to do it.

Wading through buckets of human body fluids like semen, coagulated blood, vaginal secretions, amniotic fluids, saliva and detached human body parts may sound great, but it's not all fun and games. It's not as glamorous as it sounds and doesn't pay nearly what you'd expect. The average DTS decon crew member makes between $35,000 to $60,000 a year. In busy metropolitan areas with high crime rates, you can earn as much as $100,000. Of course, few actually see that much money because the average career span of a decontamination cleaner is less than 8 months, so you have to figure that in with the unemployment you'll be collecting after you leave.

So, I asked myself, "Do I have what it takes to be a decontamination cleaner?" I think I do. After all, I've seen my share of kids puking outside of bars. I've even changed a nasty diaper or two. But, there's a big difference between changing grandma's urine-soaked sheets and scraping intestines off of a ceiling fan.

The two most important requirements for becoming a DTS decon team member are having a strong stomach and being able to show empathy toward family members during a crisis. Some people find extracting bone fragments out of the front of a television while eating lunch a bit unsettling. It's just part of the job. And crew members need to be able to express tender, loving responses to a grieving member of the family when they ask why you won't let them have a look at Uncle Nestor.

Training to become a DTS decon crew member involves several types of instruction. The first part is performed online using a computer, where new students can experience the thrill of the smell and feel of a fresh crime scene from the comfort of their home. To enhance the experience, students can watch specially prepared DVDs that explain in detail how to navigate a slippery crime scene, what to do if you find someone hiding in the closet with a shotgun aimed at your head and how to dispose of illegal drugs (the legal way).

The final part of training is hands-on. During hands-on training, the instructors set up a real-life scenario like, "We have a shotgun suicide to take care of and we want you to come with us. Newman, I want you to take care of the drapes. Clarke, I want you to clear a way through the laundry room. Don't forget your shovels and buckets." Adequate time is allowed for vomiting inside your hazmat suit and running, screaming away from the crime scene as you determine that there are easier ways to make a living.

Every professional dresses in task-specific uniforms and uses special gear. The DTC decon team member dresses in disposable, bio-hazard suits from head to toe, sealed with duct tape. Cleaners don filtered respirators and wear rubber gloves and booties before entering the crime scene. Along with their uniforms, they'll bring the tools of their trade: 55-gallon plastic containers, sponges, mops, enzyme solvents, putty knives and shovels. The last two items are particularly useful for scraping various forms of excrement and coagulated blood off the ceilings, walls and floors that has turned to the consistency of Jell-O. After the contaminated tissues have been scoured from the rooms, they'll be carefully bagged and labeled as hazardous waste material and transported to medical waste incinerators—all at additional cost to the client.

After graduating from DTS decon school, you're ready for your first real test—usually the scene of a violent crime that has been picked over by the police, fire department and crime scene investigators who have all done their jobs and departed, leaving everything else for you.

The police will meet with the decontamination lead and inform them of the risks of the crime scene—risks like decomposing bodies. If Grandma died a month ago underneath her electric blanket, she will be in a state of "decomp." During decomp, the body swells, the skin liquefies and maggots move in to feed off the body. But this all pales in comparison to the smell as ammonia gas fills the room. And if this doesn't make you consider giving up and going back to being a driving instructor, consider that all of the insects and maggots that made Grandma's body their home, must be rounded up and destroyed to eliminate bio-hazard threats.

So, if you're looking for a challenging, well-paying job that involves gaining the respect of other professionals while working under a variety of conditions, becoming a member of a CTS Decon team could be for you. Unfortunately, it wasn't for me.

Living the Streamlined Life

I'm not working these days, so it's hard for me to believe that anyone could possibly be short on time. By the time I roll out of the sack, amble downstairs to get the newspaper and finish my breakfast, it's almost noon. But, I do remember the days when things were different—rising before 6:00, showering, shaving, trimming my nose hairs, making my lunch, taking out the garbage, walking the dog, picking up after the dog, dropping off the dry cleaning and stopping by Starbucks—all in the hour before the staff meeting begins.

The infrequent days when I was relieved of any of these duties was such a relief. Yippee! Fifteen more minutes of sleep. So, I started wondering if there wasn't a more efficient way to organize my day. Just by not picking up the dog poop, I could spend 15 more minutes at the office, Skyping my friends in Singapore.

According to a 2005 study conducted by Salary.com, the average American worker admits to frittering away over two hours a day cruising the web, shopping for clothes, updating their status on Facebook and generally spacing out. If I could come up with just a few ways to economize on my daily activities, I could spend an extra hour on Twitter, letting everyone know that I'm not doing anything.

Most families (especially with kids) do all of their grocery shopping once or twice a week. A few even go every day. To save time, try doing all of your food shopping for the entire year in one visit. Naturally, this takes a lot more planning and space, but it can save you over 39 hours a year. Be prepared to drag along a heftier shopping list (104 loaves of bread, 36 chickens, 150 lbs. of hamburger meat and 26 cases of chili), enlist the kids to help you push the ten additional shopping carts you'll need and rent a small commercial van at Ryder Trucks to haul it all home.

An even better alternative to shopping for yourself is to have your food delivered, saving you gasoline, wear and tear on your auto batteries, tune-ups and new tires. Jump on Amazon.com and go to the Grocery & Gourmet Food section and let your mouse do the walking. Try restricting all of your meals to foods you can heat up instead of making from scratch. On Mondays, you can have pizza; Tuesdays, Fried Chicken TV dinners; Wednesdays, Wing Foo's Chinese food, etc. After a while, you'll find that there's absolutely no reason to leave the house just to buy food.

Most busy homemakers prepare their families' lunches the old fashioned way: a fresh sandwich every morning. At fifteen minutes per lunch, this one activity accounts for over 12.5 hours of wasted time per year. Here's a great alternative: try making a whole year's worth of lunches at one time. Instead of making 3 sandwiches every day for you and the kids, make 720 sandwiches at one time, throw them into 720 brown paper bags with 720 apples, 720 bags of chips and 720 boxes of juice. If you follow the previous tip by shopping ahead, this will fit in perfectly with your schedule. On busy mornings, skip the lunches and send the kids to school with a roll of quarters for the vending machines.

Making coffee every morning is also very inefficient—but we do need the caffeine. So, instead of making one pot every morning, try buying a 100-cup coffee urn. You know, the kind they have at PTA meetings? Make 100 cups, three times a year and all you'll have to do is re-warm them in the microwave each morning, shaving valuable minutes off of your morning.

Another useful alternative to preparing and eating three meals a day is to load up with one large meal, the first thing in the morning. This meal should be at least 2500—3000 calories—the caloric equivalent of all of your daily meals rolled into one. The idea is if you eat one huge meal at 7:00 in the morning, you'll feel so bloated and uncomfortable, you won't feel like eating for the rest of the day. This idea works especially well on Thanksgiving Day.

According to a study conducted by the University of West England, the average worker spends more than 139 hours a year commuting to and from the office, resulting in higher levels of stress, uncontrolled blood pressure, fatigue at work, lower back pain, difficulty focusing on simple tasks, anger management problems and lost time on Facebook. Wouldn't it be great if you could reclaim those 139 hours and work more efficiently? Well, you can—by working at home.

By asking your boss for the opportunity to work from home, you'll enjoy a number of immediate benefits. First, you won't have to wear clothes, so it will cut down on your laundry (see discussion below). You'll also save money by dispensing with a number of personal products like shaving cream, toothpaste, deodorant, mouthwash, shampoo, etc. Since no one will be around you all day, there's no point in showering or taking part in other unnecessary hygienic rituals. If you can manage to work from bed, you'll also cut down on the number of calories that you expend by walking through the house, allowing you to skip meals and eliminating even more groceries.

How many hours would you estimate that you waste every week doing laundry? Five, ten, fifteen? If you can get permission to work from home, you can do away with washing all underwear, bras, T-shirts, panties, sport shirts, blue jeans, socks, turtlenecks, girdles and ascots. The only article of clothing that you'll have to wash will be your dressing gown and you can have your wife do that while you're sleeping. Another helpful hint is to eliminate washable clothing altogether. Try stopping at your local medical supply warehouse and purchase a case of disposable hospital gowns. At the end of your work day, simply toss them away!

Exercising causes you to sweat, which means that you'll have to take a shower. That's a lot of wasted water and energy going down the drain. Exercising also causes you to burn unnecessary calories. It encourages you to eat more, resulting in wasted time and money with food preparation and grocery shopping (see discussions above). If you feel that you absolutely must exercise, try to save it all for one event—like jogging to your daughter's wedding.

There are a number of other routines that will save you countless hours over the course of a year. First, estimate how much your annual utilities will be and pay them all in advance. Do the same thing for your mortgage payments, car payments, income taxes and Elks Club dues. If you have trouble coming up with that much cash at once, sell your car, take out a home equity loan or put your three-year-old son to work. Another thing you can do is learn to delegate. Give your wife all of the unsavory tasks to complete like fixing the garbage disposal and changing the oil so you'll still have time to watch Oprah.

Speaking in Tongues

Long before technology made everything more complex and difficult to learn, it was easy to fix things around the house. With a toolkit from Sears & Roebuck, I could cajole, jimmy or duct tape just about anything into working order—at least long enough to haul it off to someone else who really knew what they were doing. Nowadays, I would no sooner try to change the oil in my truck than perform grandma's root canal in the kitchen with a pair of French fry tongs.

Things have gotten complicated. Plumbers, mechanics, dentists and computer geeks spend years in the classroom, learning their own language. Make the mistake of asking them "what's wrong" with your lawnmower, blender or station wagon and they'll reply with an explanation that will leave you in the dust faster than a Czech tour guide.

After getting a deal on a used refrigerator, I called a plumber to connect the automatic ice maker for me. While inspecting the fridge, he let out a long, low whistle and confessed, "Well, I can go ahead and connect the ice maker for you, but it'll be expensive. When they delivered the refrigerator, they bent the female Stratten joint leading to the anode rod, causing the thermocoupler to rub against the angle stop. Now, I can do one of two things: I can replace the T & P valve and the no-hub connector—which means that the ice maker will make cubes non-stop, 24 hours a day—or I can redirect the Descanso fitting so that it's more in line with the external flashing. That should allow the closet auger to fit properly against the yoke vent, but the work will cost you three times what the refrigerator is worth."

Last summer I decided I'd enjoy the warm summer evenings more with a slightly larger deck outside the back door. So, I scheduled a general contractor to come over to bid on extending the deck three feet. After an hour, he came back with a clipboard jammed with disheveled paperwork and his summary: "This is a beautiful piece of land you have here—unfortunately, your entire foundation is built on quicksand, so it's not appropriate for a deck. But, we can still do it if you're willing to pay for a new balloon wall, with imported Teak joists that scissor truss to a story pole and are batten cleated to a cat's paw. We can reinforce the high traffic areas with cripple rafters dovetailed into dado joints, secured with fishplates and flashing. Shouldn't cost more than $45,000."

A week later, I decided to take my beloved 1965 Chevy to one of our local mechanics to have him replace the clutch. After leaving the car with him for a day and a half, I finally got a call from him in middle of the afternoon. "Hello. This is Bruce at Olag's Grease Academy. I have some good news and bad news about your Chevy," he said.

"I looked at all of the usual things like the bead seats, the caster shims, Remington bolts, CV joints, the cycling orifice tube, the torque converter valve and the variable control relay modules," said Bruce. "They all need to be replaced—that's the good news. The bad news is that the only dealer where they stock the parts is in Akron, Ohio, so it will take a few days to ship them here. And since they celebrate Akron Museum Days from the 17th through the 20th, they probably won't arrive until next Friday."

"After we replace those," said Bruce, "We'll probably have to look around for after-market components for the airflow sensor, ambient compressor switch, ballast resistor and Cardan joints. Of course, that still leaves replacing the McPherson struts, the control vacuum regulator, the EGR valve position sensor and the mixture control solenoid. That should help the power to weight ratio but may mean we'll have to machine the Bokelman coupler and the three-way Johnson converter. And at this altitude, that usually means that we'll need to replace and recalibrate the sub-oxygen sensor, the airflow modulator and the high swirl combustion recycler. Hopefully that should do it. Should I go ahead?"

The dentist's office is one of those places where I'll go in for a simple teeth cleaning, but leave with the understanding that I need my entire jaw reconstructed. Regardless how good my oral hygiene is, I always learn that I never brush, floss, gargle or water pique enough.

Dentists always soften you up with a pretty, compassionate dental hygienist who leaves her top two buttons unfastened. After a few minutes of poking and prodding, she'll ask, "Have you been flossing every day?" I'll rebound with, "No, have you been doing your push-ups?"

After thirty more minutes of scraping, scratching and probing ("Does it hurt when I shove this ice pick and inch into your bleeding gum line?"), you're ready for the full orthodontic treatment: a check-up, an occlusal radiograph, tooth whitening, bite wing x-rays and acid etching. After the smoke and smell of burnt flesh has cleared, Dr. Kutchapekkeroff is ready to see you.

"Good morning," said Dr. Kutchapekkeroff. "Well, Nadja has cleaned your teeth and taken a full set of x-rays, so I thought we'd discuss what we found." Gulp.

"Your deciduous teeth are still present and have worn thin—down to their pulp chambers—which puts you at risk for abscesses and sepsis. So, they're going to have to come out right away. We can probably save your second bicuspid tooth on the left side, but the rest will have to be extracted and replaced with implants. I also noticed severe periodontal disease around the entire lower left quadrant—particularly near your impacted wisdom teeth. That's probably why people tell you that your breath is so bad."

"You have a number of torn fenums and half a dozen nicked molars from opening beer cans with your teeth," said Dr. Kutchapekkeroff. "The interproximal gaps between all of your teeth are preventing the growth of osteoblasts and osteoclasts, so I recommend that you see a periodontist as soon as possible. With a little luck, we should be able to irrigate and decontaminate the affected areas without having to immobilize your lower jaw—or at least until we can correct your occlusal plane. You'll be wearing an external appliance for six months until we can fly in a TMJ specialist from Switzerland to further study your condition. By the way, what kind of dental insurance do you have?"

Just when I recovered from all of my other catastrophes, my computer crashed. Since I use my PC for hourly updates on Facebook, it's imperative that I keep it in tip top condition.

Modern computers are the opposite of me. They're smaller, lighter, more powerful and capable of making millions of decisions in a second. I, on the other hand am larger, heavier, weaker and have trouble remembering where I left my retainer. And, they're almost impossible to repair yourself. After spending hours on the phone with a support technician in India trying to diagnose the sound coming from the back of the fan, I decided to bite the bullet and take it into the shop. "Can you leave it with me for a month?" asked Darpeep.

Four days later, I received a call from Darpeep—he had fixed the problem. "The problem turned out to be a little more complex than I thought," he said. "I couldn't pin down the explosions and the sparks flying out the back of the CPU when I turned it on, so I replaced the power supply with an Ultra X3 ULT 24,000 watt dual channel power supply with a 135mm fan and SLI CrossFire certifications. It's the same power supply that they use to launch the space shuttle. Of course, there wasn't enough room to mount it, so I had to remove two PCI expansion slots. To do that, I had to swap out the entire motherboard and repopulate it with new video, sound and network cards, replace all of the SCSI controllers and upgrade the BIOS."

"Since I had gone that far," he said, "I thought I might as well replace and defrag the hard drives for better access time and partition it into its native configuration to speed up the print spooler. Things worked pretty well until I discovered that the heat sink was melting through the plastic case, so I replaced it with a top of the line, water-cooled heat sink. You'll have to get in touch with your plumber to run a water line into your office. Oh, and you'll also need to buy a new monitor. I toasted the old one."

At first, I used to try to understand what they were all talking about by buying books on computers, kitchen appliances, auto repair and advanced dental procedures, but eventually I just gave up. The technicians are working harder than I am to keep me in the dark. After all . . . that's how they make their living, right?

Ripped from the Headlines

For Better or for Worse

Boston, Massachusetts—In a landmark case for matrimonial rights, a Boston man married himself today in a private service. Roland Nigland, 31, stood before a municipal judge and a small gathering of close friends to profess his love to himself in what is believed to be the first same-person marriage on record.

"From the moment that I saw my reflection in the mirror," said Nigland, "I fell in love with myself." Nigland confessed that the first time that he started to experience strong feelings for himself was in the third grade. "I snuck into my room the other morning and pressed my nose into a hamper of my dirty laundry. I just couldn't get that fragrance out of my mind." As Nigland became a young man, he started to experience undeniable sexual feelings for himself. "At first, I tried to ignore them. But, one day when my hand innocently brushed up against my thigh, I knew that I had to take it to the next level."

In the beginning, Nigland harmlessly flirted with himself in the school library, but feared that someone might catch him in the act, so he started renting cheap rooms at the Bedford Motel. "I was always nervous when I checked in. I began to sweat when the desk clerk asked me how many guests would be spending the night—even though I knew it was only me. Sometimes I'd just pay double to avoid causing suspicion."

After several years of clandestine meetings, Nigland finally decided to come out of the closet. At dinner one evening, he confessed to his parents that he was in love with himself and that he was making plans to marry. His parents were stunned. "What about that attractive Elaine Lieberman down the street?" exclaimed his mother. "And what about starting a family?" Nigland tried explaining to his parents that after years of futilely dating others, he realized that there was only one person for him: himself. And as far as a starting a family—well, he'd try, but there was always adoption if he couldn't get pregnant.

Now that the pressure was off, Nigland finally began to openly enjoy the pleasure of his own company. He could walk down the street, holding his hand in his. He could snuggle against his own shoulder. He could whisper sexual innuendos and play with himself underneath the dinner table. When confronted by friends, he didn't have to fabricate excuses about his missing date. Instead, people began to accept him as a couple. There were other benefits, too.

"When I used to date women, I'd always have to wait around for them while they got dressed, wondering how long it would be until they'd be ready. Now, when I'm getting dressed for a night out on the town, I always know exactly how long it will be until I'm ready to go." Nigland brought up a number of other benefits with marrying yourself. "For years, I racked my brains over what would be the appropriate birthday or Christmas gift for my girlfriend. Well, those days are over. Now, whenever I buy a gift for myself, it's exactly what I want, the right size and color. And no more guessing what's in the little box underneath the Christmas tree!"

And what about the sex? "Unbelievable," said Nigland. "Last year on vacation in Hawaii, I booked a suite at the Fairmont Orchid and had a magnum of Champaign sent up to my room—just to surprise myself. I was absolutely stunned. After a fabulous dinner, I hopped over the threshold (since I couldn't really carry myself) and spent the evening caressing and pleasuring myself. I've never had sex like that with a woman!"

What's in Nigland's future? "I hope to inspire other men and women to marry themselves. Think about how much a movement like this could impact the staggering divorce rates. Why, we'd cut it down to nil."

He's also thinking about establishing a foundation to support others who would like to marry themselves. "I'd like to set up the 'Roland Nigland Half-way House for Self-lovers' so that they won't have to suffer the same indignities that I did. I'm also thinking of starting a new clothing line called 'I Love Me So Much' that will feature pants, shirts, sweaters and blouses that are reversible; one side for each of you." For more information about how you can marry yourself, visit www.ILoveMeSoMuch.com.

Hot Careers for 2011

Washington, D.C.—As the national unemployment rate skyrocketed to over 8%, authorities remain concerned over the number of able-bodied men and women unable to find gainful employment. "It's getting really tough out there. Even for college graduates," said Wilton Fraleigh, U.S. Labor Secretary.

"People who have depended on their education and experience are finding it necessary to come up with more creative career solutions," said Nicola Speranza, Career Counselor at Isaias Scrichfield Community College in Pumpkin Center, Missouri. So, to solve the problem, the Obama Administration has published its annual list of hot careers in an effort to get Americans back to work. Here is a brief list of the most sought after professions for 2011.

Colonic Hydrotherapy Technician—Many chiropractors, naturopaths and assorted practitioners believe that the inside of the digestive tract is the mirror to the soul. So, to keep it springtime fresh, Colonic Hydrotherapy Technicians flush more than 20 gallons of water, herbs, enzymes and coffee through thirty inches of rubber hose, up where the sun don't shine. Training consists of 100 hours of intensive online training and X-Box simulations followed by a final examination where examinees administer treatments to one another.

Odor Judge—Ever wonder how your favorite antiperspirant made it from the test tube to your underarm? Odor Judges are faced with the daunting task of evaluating thousands of scents under a variety of real life situations to determine which products perform the best under stressors such as a first date, obtaining a learner's permit or surviving a job interview. Odor Judges must complete 1500 hours of training that includes anatomy, physiology, biochemistry and scent identification.

Mortuary Beautician—Three days after Auntie Bernice leaves this earth, she'll be viewed by every member of her extended family and a thousand people she never met, so it's important that she look her best. The Mortuary Beautician is charged with instilling the healthy glow that the embalmer removed. The Mortuary Beautician is responsible for makeup, hairstyling and wardrobe coordination of the recently deceased. In cases where the deceased has met with a violent death, Mortuary Beauticians fill in the bullet holes, stab wounds and reassemble the body parts to make the departed look like their old self again. Most Mortuary Beauticians start out as beauty school dropouts or auto body repairmen.

Human Cannonball—For those interested in shooting for the stars, a career as a Human Cannonball can be the bullet train to success. Employed at circuses and traveling carnivals, Human Cannonballs enjoy a variety of working environments and are in great demand in the entertainment industry. Prerequisites include a slim physique, an appreciation of high power ordinance and a love of high places.

Breast Measurer—One of the most popular new careers this year often glossed over by high school career counselors is the Breast Measurer. Since the seventh century BC, women have been plagued with poor fitting brassieres, often resulting in maceration, intertrigo and upper back pain. Up until recently, women have depended on a system of trial and error to properly fit bras. Recent scientific measuring approaches have also fallen short. For the professional Breast Measurer, measurement techniques depend on a key sense of touch using the palm of the hand and fingertips to measure the weight, volume and circumference of the breast resulting in more accurate measurements. There is currently a five-year backlog of applications for schools offering this curriculum

Automobile Repossessors—Ever dreamed of driving the finest luxury automobiles without being saddled by huge car payments? Then perhaps repossessing cars is for you! Automobile Repossessors assist banks, credit unions and car dealerships with reclaiming their assets from individuals unable to make their scheduled car payments. Automobile Repossessors enjoy an action packed lifestyle as deadbeat creditors assault them with a variety of firearms, knives and other high speed projectiles. Medical insurance is strongly recommended.

Ant Catcher—You'll never forget the look on your child's face the first time you see them studying an army of red ants burrowing a path to nowhere between two panes of glass in the comfort of your living room—ants that you've caught yourself! Ant Catchers enjoy a variety of work environments like crawl spaces under houses, parched desert landscapes and automobile junkyards. Catching ants requires a minimum amount of training and an infinite amount of patience.

Egg Breaker—Have you ever ordered an "egg white only" omelet? Ever wondered just who removed the yolks? Egg Breakers separate the yolks and whites of eggs for use in food products by striking eggs against a bar, then pouring the contents of the broken eggs into an egg-separating device. Egg Breakers enjoy the fast paced life of the professional kitchen staff and are employed in fast food restaurants, bakeries, soup kitchens and federal penitentiaries.

Ball Picker—If you enjoy wandering aimlessly around in circles looking at the ground, then you'll thrill to the excitement of spending your days picking up used golf balls from fairways, putting greens and from the bottom of slime-infested duck ponds. Ball Pickers enjoy a flexible work schedule and an independent lifestyle in a variety of locations from private golf courses to community driving ranges. Ball Pickers should be comfortable with constant bending at the waist, handling filthy objects and wading into shallow, alligator-infested, murky bodies of water.

Chicken Sexer—Chicken Sexers are highly trained individuals charged with the task of separating male chicks from female chicks. Male chickens are used primarily for their meat, while female chickens are used for their egg production. Chicken Sexers are trained in two techniques: Feather Sexing and Vent Sexing. Professional Feather Sexers can quickly determine the sex of a male chick by observing their long, wing pinfeathers. Vent Sexing involves literally squeezing the poop out of the chicks until their rectums dilate, allowing the Chicken Sexer to observe a small bump in the male chicks. Chicken Sexers must be ambidextrous and possess superior grip strength.

Wrinkle Chaser—Wrinkle Chasers iron wrinkles from leather shoes during their manufacture to ensure they are perfectly smooth before the customer purchases them. They spend up to 15 hours a day on their feet, with their hands immersed in toxic chemicals used to treat leather. Some famous celebrities who once worked as Wrinkle Chasers include Tamar Olverson, Geraldo Tipold , Siobhan Fattore and Whitney Holtgrefe.

Rent Boy—If you're an attractive, well-endowed man interested in working from your own home while making big money, then a career as a Rent Boy could be for you. Rent Boys serve the sexual needs of successful women between the ages of 30-85 by supplying massages, cross-dressing, stripteases, sexual role playing and offering something that their clients' rich and successful husbands can't (or won't). Rent boys generally work from 1—3 hours per appointment, several times a week. Premium rates are charged for sexual proficiency, good looks and for servicing plumper clients. Rental rates strictly adhere to NFRB (National Federation of Rent Boys) guidelines.

Manure Inspector—One and a half billion tons of manure are produced by animals in this country each year—90 percent of it from cattle. Animal manure is loaded with contaminants like campylobacter, salmonella and E.coli which can cause kidney failure in children and painful, bloody diarrhea in everyone else. Manure Inspectors are charged with extracting these bacteria from animals and facilitating methods to eliminate them from our food. Manure Inspectors enjoy the freedom of working independently, free of petty meddling by upper level management.

Semen Washer—Thanks to semen washers (and in vitro fertilization), more than 250,000 babies have been delivered in the U.S. since 1995. Semen Washers analyze seminal goo, placing samples under a microscope to perform sperm counts. After washing, Semen Washers spin the samples to separate the plasma from the motile cells. Following processing, the samples are carted off to freezers for up to twenty years. Semen Washers typically work late night shifts in medical laboratories or black market sperm banks.

Orangutan Pee Collector—Orangutan Pee Collectors monitor the steroid, estrogen, progesterone, cortisol and ketone levels of primate urine through non-invasive measurements for a variety of scientific purposes. Information about an Orangutan's levels of stress and their reproductive cycle can be determined by carefully measuring and tasting their diddle. Orangutan Pee Collectors must possess a Ph.D. in molecular biology, superior eye sight and a heightened sense of smell.

Jelly Doughnut Filler—Many consumers are surprised to learn that jelly doughnuts do not come out of the oven filled with jelly. To the contrary, jelly doughnuts leave the oven as solid, doughy globs of baked flour. The jelly is introduced into the donut by a specially trained technician who plunges a large hypodermic needle into the side of the donuts, then pumps the goo in by hand. Jelly Doughnut Fillers generally have superior upper body strength, must be able to tolerate hours of repetitious labor, high fat diets and hours spent on their feet. A college education is not required.

Lifeguard at a Nude Beach—Looking for a way to put all of those wasted hours of lying around the house naked to good use? Then life guarding at a nude beach could be for you! Nude Beach Lifeguards enjoy the slow paced, yet highly charged lifestyle that is the envy of every young man and woman. Nude Beach Lifeguards generally possess low hormone levels and uncompromising self control. Applicants must have 20/20 vision, be certified in advanced lifesaving, cardiopulmonary resuscitation and basic anatomy. No uniform is required.

Stand-in Bridesmaid—Anyone who's ever been to a poorly attended wedding can attest to the embarrassment of the wedding party when a paltry showing occurs—especially at the alter. Stand-in Bridesmaids satisfy the growing need for pseudo-friends after their social circles have been annihilated by drug addiction, arrest warrants, restraining orders, infidelity and divorce. Stand-in Bridesmaids may be rented individually, in pairs or by the six-pack. Special deals may also be arranged for stand-in grooms, mothers, fathers, best men and entire wedding parties.

Bingo Board Announcer—When was the last time that you experienced the thrill of being the first one in the room to fill up an empty Bingo card? If it's been a while, then the exciting world of Bingo Board Announcing is waiting for you! Bingo Board Announcers enjoy working in a variety of interesting settings that include Veteran Administration Hospitals, managed care facilities, Elks Clubs, insane asylums and dialysis clinics. No college degree is required, but prospective announcers must be able to count from 1 to 10 without using their fingers and be familiar with the American alphabet.

Piercing Technician—The first time that your teenage daughter came home with a metal stud jutting from the left side of her nostril, you probably thought to yourself, "Dang, I wish I could have done that to my little girl." Well, now you can. Body Piercing is one of the fastest growing careers for displaced middle managers, aerospace engineers, computer programmers and other college-educated professionals. All you need to get started in this lucrative field is a reasonably good aim, poor taste and a familiarity with hardware.

Don't let that college education come between you and your perfect job. Start thinking outside of the box and join the millions of Americans who enjoy the fast-paced lifestyle of today's alternative careers!

Sticky Bomb Threat Foiled

Los Angeles, California—American authorities announced yesterday that they had successfully thwarted an attempt by terrorists to detonate dozens of "sticky bombs" made from 1-liter bottles of Diet Coke and Mentos candy mints, preventing what could have been the messiest attack on U.S. air carriers in aviation history.

The Transportation Security Administration first became aware of the threat after observing a number of men of Middle Eastern descent carrying cases of the popular drink onto six different planes. "At first, we were focused on what was in their carry-on luggage," said Henry Wilkinson, TSA's Chief of Domestic Terrorism. "We were looking for mainstream explosives like jelled nitroparafin, metal perchlorate and nitroglycerin. It never even dawned on us to look for soda." Security officials at Los Angeles International Airport let the men breeze right through the screening stations, completely unaware of the threat they represented.

The bombs were made from a number of very simple, yet deadly components. The men, all in their early twenties and members of the radical "al-Quesadilla" extremist group, first became aware of the soda's volatile nature after visiting the "Professor Brainius Wild and Wacky Science for Kids" website, where it explained in detail how to explode liters of Diet Coke by dropping packages of Mentos mints into them. "The Diet Coke idea was brilliant," said Wilkinson. "They knew that they could easily smuggle the Mentos on board by stringing them together and wearing them around their necks as Afghan fertility beads," said Wilkinson. "Then, they stuffed 12, one liter bottles of Diet Coke into the inside pockets of their wool trench coats." The fact that it was mid-August and over 100 degrees outside, failed to generate any interest from the TSA agents or passengers—even during a pat down. Once on-board, assembling the bombs was easy.

President Obama was on vacation at Camp David when Department of Homeland Security Secretary, Janet Napolitano informed him of the threat. The President then called Prime Minister David Cameron, who was on vacation in the Caribbean, who in turn called Russian President Dmitry Medvedev who ironically, was also on vacation. This continued for several hours until Prince Albert of Monaco was finally reached, who called Werner Beltram, Assistant Under-Secretary of Parks and Recreation for Lichtenstein: apparently the only government official from a major country who was actually in his office working.

The terrorists were all of Pakistani origin, living in the United States under work visas issued by Piggy Wiggly Markets, Inc. This gave them unfettered access to the soda and mints. When questioned about how they learned to make such lethal, dangerous bombs, Al-man Rajeem Nadwaz Korumi Ami Haabat, the leader of the group said, "We spent years learning how to handle volatile high explosives in Libyan, Pakistani and Syrian training camps. For the Mentos bombs, we just looked on the back of the bottles."

As a result of the scare, all incoming and outgoing flights were cancelled throughout the United States, with the exception of the Sitka, Tweed-Newhaven, Magic Valley, Kalamazoo/Battlecreek, Sloulin Field and Pago Pago airports. Foot traffic came to a screeching halt at the Pirates of the Caribbean ride in Orlando, Florida where members of the public were forced to succumb to random strip searches. Even the space shuttle Endeavor was instructed to abort its landing at Kennedy Space Center and return to Mars. "We've put the country on 'Condition Red'," said Napolitano. "As a result of the events that transpired in Los Angeles, we're removing all soda and candy machines from airports, train stations and bus depots across the U.S. You just can't be too careful."

White House Press Secretary, Jay Carney, announced in this morning's press briefing, "Let me assure you, it is perfectly safe to travel in America—just not in aircraft, trains, motorcycles, cruise ships, aircraft carriers, zeppelins, wheelbarrows, hot-air balloons, lunar rovers, rickshaws, aerial tramways, funiculars, horse drawn chariots, heavy cruisers, outrigger canoes, conveyor belts, escalators, battleships, Amish buggies, Naval destroyers,

8-man skulls, inner tubes, shopping carts, bicycles, pogo sticks or civilian motor vehicles. Unicycles are fine."

President Obama called the thwarted plot, " . . . a stark reminder of the lengths that extremists will go to try to disrupt the lives of innocent citizens." TSA Director, Kip Hawley, pledged to get things moving again as quickly as possible. "During the past 10 years, we have asked the public to help us with the screening process by leaving all Bowie knives, spears, switchblades, hunting rifles, Claymore mines, swords, patriot missiles, shotguns, crossbows, slingshots, taser guns, scissors, nunchuks, nail files, ballpoint pens, bullwhips, surgical scalpels, C4 explosives, staplers, 3-hole punches, blasting caps, wireless detonating devices and dynamite at home."

"This morning," said Hawley, "I'm going ask everyone to go just one step further and wear hospital gowns when they fly. Leave all of your luggage at home—both checked and carry-on. This will make it much easier during the check-in process."

By Tuesday, travelers at our nation's airports began to see things return to normal. The check-in lines were back to their usual three-hour wait and people were happily arguing with TSA agents again. "I feel perfectly safe flying," said Kyoshi Katate, 24, who was on her way back to Cosmetology school in Japan. "It's been a little strange learning to fly without any luggage or underwear, but I'm starting to get used to it."

Steroids Invade the World of Professional Chess

Canton, Ohio—The professional chess world was rocked today when 13-year-old chess prodigy, Bobby Baines, was disqualified from play for testing positive for steroids.

Clayton Groman, Director of the United States Chess Federation announced during a press conference from his office in Crossville, Tennessee that Baines was one of 17 professional chess players ranging in ages from 8 to 97 years old that are under suspicion for taking performance enhancing drugs on the USCF list of banned substances.

"We've had Mr. Baines in our crosshairs for quite some time," said Groman. "We first became suspicious when we noticed that he was becoming much more violent during matches and began exhibiting impaired judgment stemming from feelings of invincibility." During one recent chess match, Baines became upset over his opponent's delay in play, so he leaped over the table, hoisted him up into an Airplane Spin and threw him into the audience.

"He's just a boy," pleaded Bobby's mother and manager, Agatha Baines. "Like all boys his age, he's bound to make mistakes." When asked if she noticed any other recent changes in Bobby, Agatha confessed that she had noticed some small, yet noticeable physical changes in her son over the past six months. "For one thing, he started to grow more hair—a lot of hair." she said. "I'm well aware that boys entering puberty are likely to experience changes in their bodies, but I saw Bobby in the shower one afternoon and his back was absolutely covered with hair. He looked just like my brother, Leo and he's 67-years-old. But what really alarmed me was when I saw Bobby trimming the hair in his ears. He's only 13 for God's sake." She also confessed to witnessing some rather rapid weight gain in Bobby. "He gained over 35 pounds of muscle in one week," she said. "We had to stop buying his clothes at Oshkosh B'Gosh and start shopping at Eagleson's Big and Tall Shop for Men."

After hours of fierce interrogation by USCF investigators, Baines refused to reveal the source of the illegal steroids at Our Lady of Hubert Junior High School. Even depriving him of his Nintendo after school and making him eat the Mac &Cheese in the student cafeteria failed to yield any worthwhile information. When questioned about the bottles of Androstenedione, Primobolan, Tetrahydrogestrinone, Clenbuterol and DHA police found in his backpack, Baines finally caved in and said, "I got them from a vending machine outside the boys' locker room. Originally, I thought they were Mentos, but they tasted awful and made me feel funny. Later, when I saw what they were doing for my chess game, I got hooked."

"Parents and coaches just don't understand how much pressure we're under to perform," said Baines. "All of the young chess players are just so big and powerful, these days. I have to take steroids just to stay competitive." Groman confirmed Baines' comments. "Five years ago, a normal 13 year old boy would be around 5 foot 4 and weigh about 100 pounds. Today, that's all changed. Bobby routinely has matches against other boys his age who are 6 foot 2 and weight over 235."

"I need these drugs to compete," cried Baines.

Drug abuse and doping is nothing new in the world of professional chess. In 1973, Grand Master Valery Solov was suspended for 14 games after blood tests confirmed a hematocrit of over 67%. After months of deliberation, Solov finally confessed to blood doping as part of a plea deal that resulted in the restoration of his tournament privileges. "I was scheduled to play a particularly brutal tournament in Denver, Colorado," said Solov. "They call Denver 'the Mile High City' and I needed to do whatever I could to be at my best at that altitude. I admit I was wrong. But everybody's doing it."

"Part of Bobby's problem is the lousy role models that teens have these days," said Jessie Stagg, Bobby's third period physical education teacher. "They see professional athletes like Barry Bonds and Jose Canseco doing steroids to pump up their batting averages and ask themselves, 'Why shouldn't I?'"

"Even though they're only in 8ᵗʰ grade, the competition for full chess scholarships to the Ivy League colleges is incredible. Kids gotta do what they gotta do," said Stagg.

And it's not only athletics that are being impacted by performance enhancing drugs. "Steroids have absolutely destroyed our boys' voices," complained Lois Prum, Director of the St. Anthony's Boys' Choir at the Junior High School. "They used to sound so angelic. But their voices were cracking left and right at last year's Christmas Pageant. They absolutely annihilated 'Good King Wenceslas'."

The next step in the investigation is to request a Sample B of Bobby's blood from the Olympic Analytical Laboratory at the University of California, Los Angeles. "The problem with analyzing Bobby's Sample B, is the fact that a 13 year old boy's hormones are all over the place," said Donald H. Catlin, Director of the lab. "If he's been within ten miles of a copy of Penthouse or Hustler, his testosterone readings will be way, way off. It's just impossible to get accurate measurements."

Fortunately for Bobby, a chess competitor's career is much longer than, say a professional gymnast. "With the proper guidance and substance abuse counseling, even if he's suspended from tournament play for a year, it shouldn't really make much of an impact in his career," said Stagg. "He could get disqualified five or six times and still remain competitive. After all, Garry Kasparov was 47 when he retired and he didn't even know about steroids."

One for the Price of Two

Dallas, Texas—Following the recent decision by Southwest Airlines to begin enforcing their 22-year-old policy requiring overweight passengers to purchase two airline seats, a number of other companies and consumer groups have demanded that customers of size begin coughing up premium rates for their products and services.

Southwest Airlines led the charge with their policy to penalize large customers, dating back to the 1980's. According to the policy, any passenger whose derriere spills over onto the adjacent seat is required to purchase two airline tickets at the price of the original seat. Roxanne Haberstrohm, spokesperson for Southwest says, "Ninety percent of the complaints we receive from our passengers stem from being subjected to the overflow of obese passengers sitting next to them." And the problem isn't based solely on comfort, either.

Statistics from the National Center for Health Statistics indicate that the weight of the average American has been creeping up since the 1990's. More than a third of American adults over the age of 20 are obese. The Center for Disease Control and Prevention states that the average weight of American adults has ballooned by 10 pounds. The extra weight of these chubby vagabonds has translated into an additional $275 million dollar expenditure to burn more than 350 million additional gallons of jet fuel resulting in 3.8 million extra tons of carbon dioxide released into the air.

In an effort to contain the prices of airline tickets, air carriers have initiated creative ways to compensate for the additional weight of their plump passengers such as pitching out phones, carpeting on cabin floors, pillows, drop-down trays, flight attendants, light fixtures, stereo headsets, co-pilots, blankets, air conditioners, communication equipment, emergency oxygen masks, metal eating utensils, restrooms, thick magazines and even life vests and air sickness bags. Other ideas under consideration are dispensing with unnecessary Plexiglas windows and seat cushions in favor of wooden bench seats.

For years, airline passengers have had their carry-on baggage restricted to maximum dimensions. So, why not the passengers? One concept that is rapidly gaining popularity is to install people-sizers at all check-in counters: templates that resemble the outline of a normal-weight flyer. All passengers would be required to fit through them in order to qualify for a standard ticket. Can't fit through the people sizer? Buy two seats.

Still, other ideas that are being tossed around are charging passengers by the pound and restricting flights by sex. "The Federal Aviation Administration has revised its weight distribution calculations to add an additional 8% to the weight of male passengers and 18% for female passengers," says Haberstrohm. "Officials at the Dallas-Fort Worth Airport are also trying a new approach for managing the heft of their customers: they're weighing passengers at check-in and announcing their weight over the loudspeaker system." To help cut down on the cost of air travel, the FAA is also considering male only and female only flights. Female only flights would have fewer seats on-board to compensate for the higher percentage of body fat. "There's just no sense in penalizing male travelers for that extra 10 percent of female flab," says Haberstrohm.

Automobile makers have also been challenged to come up with more comfortable and durable models for their corpulent customers. "The first towing package became available in 1959," says Basil Chritton, Chief Design Engineer for General Motors. "Towing packages were originally installed on diesel trucks for the purposes of hauling fifth-wheel campers, boats and trailers. The equipment included beefed up suspension, heavy-duty transmissions and cooling systems," says Chritton. "But with the increased mass of our average consumer, we're now adding high-capacity air cleaners, auxiliary external transmission oil coolers and heavy-duty automatic locking rear differentials as standard equipment on all entry-level models of our economy cars such as the Chevrolet Aveo, Pontiac G6 and Buick Verano."

Not to be outdone by their competition, a number of foreign-made automobiles have begun arriving in the United States with the Nantucket option that includes bucket seats that are 20% wider, smaller diameter steering wheels to accommodate growing belly rolls and interiors that seat four passengers instead of the usual six. Even Hummer has gotten into the game. "Automatic-inflating tires have long been one of the hallmarks of our military vehicles," says Colonel Albert Dalrymple, U.S. Army (Ret.) now the Marketing Director for Hummer of USA. "We depended on it in the Gulf War and Desert Storm conflicts. Now, we're bringing the same technology to the consumer. When an overweight passenger slithers behind the wheel of the new 2012 H2, the tires immediately sense the increased load and inflate to 65 PSI."

Wider girth has also impacted the retail clothing industry. Since 2008, the Eddie Bauer and Lands End catalogues have begun advertising their clothing in tall, grande and venti sizes. "Due to the increased cost of raw materials, we've had to add Cetacean sizing to all of our lines," says Lakisha Lark, Director of Catalogue Products for Eddie Bauer. "Cetacean sizing adds a skosh more room and a 15% price increase to all of our products. And to help keep the cost of the material down, we're making all of the Cetacean products from recycled Army tents and commercial tarpaulins. Look for the seal of the American Obesity Association to be sure that you're getting the real thing!"

Another business that's been directly affected by America's problem with obesity is therapeutic massage. Once considered a luxury reserved for the rich and famous, therapeutic massage is now a widely accepted approach for correcting many structural, orthopedic and stress-related disorders in middle class patients. But the consumer's increase in mass has many in the business concerned. "Most of our therapists received their training on clients of normal body mass," says Jeanetta Greenweig, spokesperson for the National Certification Board for Therapeutic Massage and Bodywork (NCBTMB). "But within 18 months of entering the field, 75% of newly licensed massage therapists drop out due to carpal tunnel syndrome, circulation problems and extreme fatigue. They're just not prepared to handle the additional stress of massaging all of that blubber."

To help massage therapists deal with the increasing girth of their clients, the NCBTMB has developed a special Blowhole training certification, designed to teach massage therapists how to apply their techniques to larger clients. "Blowhole certified therapists are trained how to reduce the pace and force of massage to help reduce occupational injury and fatigue," says Greenweig. "We also advise therapists working on the obese to limit their sessions to 15 minutes instead of the usual 45. And, like many other industries, we charge a premium rate for Blowhole massages."

Other businesses affected by the increasing American mass are ski resorts, subways, shoe retailers, public swimming pools and restaurants; the list goes on and on. For the moment, most industry analysts see no end in sight. "If we've gained all of this weight within the past 16 years, what's going to happen to things like the earth's orbit in the next 20?" says Vincenzo Iacobucci, Director of the United States Geological Survey. "Are Mississippi, Alabama and Louisiana (where obesity rates are the highest in the country) going to start slowly sinking into the earth's core? We just don't know!"

The End of a Love Affair

Boston, Massachusetts—In a sad epilogue to an earlier published story, Roland Nigland, 33, has filed for divorce from himself citing irreconcilable differences. Readers may recall that Nigland, of Boston, Massachusetts became the first person to publicly profess his love for himself in what was believed to be the first same-person marriage on record.

"I honestly don't know what happened," said Nigland. "I was so much in love with myself. After the wedding, I set up house in a renovated Beacon Hill apartment, found a new job and made plans to start a family. All the usual stuff. But then, just as quickly, things began to fall apart."

After only 18 months of marriage, Nigland began noticing that he stopped communicating with himself. "I used to love to walk along the beach holding my hand in mine, reminiscing about all of the good times I had," said Nigland. "I'd stay up half the night caressing myself, laughing and giggling like a teenager. I even talked about raising a little Nigland or two. But suddenly, I stopped sharing intimate secrets with myself. Sex became more and more infrequent and there were the calls from a mysterious stranger who would hang up as soon as I answered the telephone. I began to suspect that I might be having an affair, so I hired a private investigator."

"He was pretty distraught when he first contacted me," said Elwood Leggette, Private Investigator with Kanari, Shefer and Mordechai Investigation Services. "Mr. Nigland told me that he suspected he was having an affair with himself. He complained of late nights at the office, Chapstick stains on his collar and a declining sex drive at home. It seemed pretty clear to me that he was onto something."

After three months of tailing Nigland, Leggette was unable to catch him in the throws of another lover. "I followed him to and from the office, out to dinner and to the movies. The only person I saw him with was himself. He didn't even seem to have any friends. So, we decided to terminate the investigation."

As Nigland continued to struggle through his turbulent marriage, he contacted Father Erasmo Floore, his pastor at Saint Filberto Bakalars Parish. "Roland came to me seeking advice on how he could salvage his marriage," said Floore. "Roland knew from the start that marrying himself wasn't going to be easy. After all, at the time there was quite a stigma to marrying oneself. It's not like it is today. But he seemed committed to making it work."

Father Floore recommended that Nigland start weekly counseling sessions with Sister Asuncion Fariello, the parish's marriage counselor. "Roland wrestled with a number of issues," said Fariello. "In particular, there were problems with money." Apparently, Nigland argued with himself over expensive purchases, vacations at the trendy Paranur Gandhi Leprosy Colony and daily visits to Starbucks. It got so bad that he tried setting up separate checking accounts—one for each of him. But even that didn't work.

Several months later, Nigland began suspecting that he might be having problems with drugs and alcohol. "I was always making excuses to myself for having to run out to the Loaf & Jug in the middle of the night. And, something was draining large sums of money from our bank account." One evening, Nigland found a half-empty bottle of Manischewitz wine squirreled away in one of his ski boots in the garage. "I confronted myself about the drinking. At first, I denied having a problem, but finally conceded that things had gotten out of hand and agreed to go into therapy." Nigland thought he had finally made significant progress towards saving his marriage. That is, until the physical abuse began.

One evening during a particularly heated discussion over a duvet cover, Nigland slapped himself across the face. "I just lost it. I couldn't believe that I would do that to myself. I started crying and locked myself in the bathroom." The next day, Nigland filed a restraining order against himself. "That was a pretty tough order to fill," lamented Sergeant Rodney Bolinger of the Boston Police Department. "What the restraining order said was that Mr. Nigland was not allowed to come within 100 yards of himself. We couldn't figure out how to enforce it." Three weeks after the order was issued, Nigland called the police complaining that he was in the same house with himself. The police took him away in handcuffs.

After months of failed attempts at reconciliation, Nigland finally filed for divorce. "I pleaded with myself. Let's try to make things work. Let's try a legal separation. At one point, I even suggested getting the marriage annulled, but I knew that the Catholic Church would never go for it. After all, I had already consummated the marriage."

With no prenuptial agreement in place, the divorce looked like it was going to be ugly. Nigland hired two attorneys; one for each side. Thankfully, there were no children from the marriage, so the battle that ensued dealt strictly with the distribution of property. After nearly six months of haggling back and forth, Nigland agreed to the conditions of Nigland. He was to get a generous monthly alimony payment if he agreed to give up his Beacon Hill apartment and the Audi.

"My life is shattered," confessed Nigland. "I really wanted the marriage to work. After all of those frustrating years of dating women, I thought I had finally found the man for me. It just goes to show that you don't really know someone until you live with them."

Sweeping Rule Changes for Competitive Eating

New York, New York—The world of competitive eating shocked the sports world yesterday when the IFOCE (International Federation of Competitive Eating) announced widespread changes to the sport of professional gurgitation.

"Due to the cutthroat nature of some of our competitors, the IFOCE has been forced to up the ante in all its sanctioned events by adding several new categories," said George Shea, Chairman of the IFOCE. In an update posted on the Federation's website, Major League Eating, Shea wrote, "Up until now, natural food products in various forms and methods of preparation were sufficient to challenge professional eaters from around the globe. But with the records falling at a startling rate, we've decided to enhance the competition by including items generally not considered food—at least in America."

What Shea is referring to is the addition of three new gustatory categories: insects & reptiles, animal sweetbreads and non-organic hardware.

The additional categories were added in an attempt to challenge the numerous eating records held for baked beans, butter, cheesecake, beef tongue, hard boiled eggs, hot dogs, buffalo wings, brats, cannoli, catfish, chili cheese fries, corned dogs, crawfish, deep-fried okra, cream filled donuts, fruitcake, garlicky greens, grits, haggis, huevos rancheros, jalapeno peppers, key lime pie, Mars Bars, meatballs, sour pickles, reindeer sausage, rocky mountain oysters and Spam. "There's one little lady named Sonya Thomas who ate over 9 pounds of Jambalaya last summer in 10 minutes," complained Shea. "Who in the hell can compete with that? And, another guy downed 45 conch fritters in less than 6 minutes! I don't know what a conch fritter is, but he ate a lot of them."

Following the success of the popular network television program, "Fear Factor," the IFOCE will begin hosting competitive events for eating insects at its next scheduled competition at Rouses World Crawfish Eating Championship in New Orleans, Louisiana. "We're going to begin by featuring three insect categories: flies, cockroaches & beetles and a miscellaneous category that includes stink bugs, caterpillars, earwigs and ticks," said Shea. "We've heard of a guy down in New Orleans, named Huc-Mazelet Luquiens, who can wolf down 72 stink bugs in 6-minutes. And there's a 24-year-old woman named Sally George Doke from Atlanta that holds the local record for South African Dung Beetles."

Early attempts with reptiles, however, have met with limited success. A reptile eating exhibition event was staged during the recent Johnsonville Bratwurst Random Drawing. "We only had two competitors. One of them got sick halfway through her Ball Python and the other one had to be carted off by paramedics after attempting to down an Inland Taipan—refuted to be one of the deadliest snakes in the world."

A more palatable event featuring animal sweetbreads will be hosted during the Waffle House World Waffle Eating Contest in Atlanta, Georgia. Last year, Joey Chestnut edged out Sonya Thomas by eating 18 1/2 eight-ounce Waffle House waffles in 10 minutes. "We'll see what they can do with bovine thymus and parotid glands. This year's contest will give some of the newcomers, already versed in sweetbread consumption, an opportunity to compete with the old timers," said Shea. "Of course, Takeru Kobayashi, past record holder for Nathan's Coney Island hot dogs already has the record for 17.7 pounds of cow brains in 15 minutes," said Shea, "But cow brains aren't generally considered sweetbreads, so that record will probably be thrown out unless we can find someone to challenge him."

The newest category to be added is the inorganic hardware category. "The hardware category is open to just about anything you might be able to find in a Home Depot and fit in your mouth," said Patrick Bertoletti, current record holder for strawberry rhubarb pie (7.9 lbs in 8 minutes on July 29, 2006). "Although it's not condoned by the IFOCE, I've been practicing with some 3/8 inch aluminum wing nuts but will probably see how I do at the Ace Hardware Labor Day IFOCE Competition with some

1/4 inch slotted pan head screws. I've heard there's a guy that works at the Lowes home improvement center in Piney Woods, Texas that can eat 27 pounds of Hexagon Flange nuts in 7 minutes. I'm sure that's some kind of record, because no one has ever done it before." Not included in the hardware category are the numerous varieties of plumber's putties, silicone caulking and window sealants.

"We're really hoping that these new categories take off and enhance not only the competitive nature or our contests, but draw more spectators to the events," said Shea. "Right now, the highest winner's purse for our events is $3,500 for the Nathan's contest. But we think if we can get sponsorship from PBS's This Old House, Sutherland's West or the Do-It-Yourself channel, we could really make it profitable for the contestants!"

The Mortuary Rose Bowl Stadium

Pasadena, California—In the continuing tradition of Fenway Park and Wrigley Field, owners of the famed Rose Bowl stadium in Pasadena, California, announced today that it is being acquired and renamed by Forest Lawn Memorial Parks & Mortuaries. The new name will be the Forest Lawn Memorial Parks & Mortuary Rose Bowl Stadium, or FLMP&MRBS (pronounced "Flemp & Merbs).

Despite a rich and colorful history, the Rose Bowl has recently fallen on hard economic times, necessitating its sale to a corporate sponsor. "We hosted our first football game on October 28, 1922, between the University of California Bears and the University of Southern California Trojans. We've been losing money ever since," said Victor Gordo, President of the Rose Bowl Operating Company. "Even though we regularly host events like the Rose Bowl, the Super Bowl, Men's and women's World Cup soccer as well as Fourth of July celebrations, concerts, religious services and the world's largest flea market, we just haven't been able to make ends meet."

Corporate sponsorship resulting in name acquisition is nothing new to the sports world. In 1953, Sportsman's Park in St. Louis was changed to Busch Stadium after the brewery bought the naming rights to the popular icon. In 1995, Candlestick Park in San Francisco was renamed 3Com Park. Since then, dozens of other stadiums around the world have traded money from corporate sponsors for naming rights. However, this is the first time that a stadium will be giving up more than just its name. Forest Lawn Memorial Parks & Mortuaries will be buying the stadium, lock, stock and barrel, resulting in a number of significant operational changes.

Beginning next year, football fans, UCLA alumni and other members of the general public will be able to purchase a traditional lawn crypt, wall crypt, sarcophagus, niche, columbarium, mausoleum or reserve space in our beautiful cremation garden," said Oscar Florianus Bluemner, Director of Sales and Marketing for Forest Lawn. "And they'll be able to do this during halftime on New Years day, a World Cup game or while taking a break at the Flea Market."

With so many other spaces available throughout the southland, a lot of people questioned the decision made by the Board of Directors of the Rose Bowl Operating Company. "The Rose Bowl has over 79,156 square feet of immaculately groomed natural turf, so it's perfect for regular ground and lawn crypts," said Richard Schammel, Director of the Pasadena Center Operating Company. "And with the huge rise in deaths occurring in southern California due to gang activity and suicides linked to unemployment, Forest Lawn is quickly running out of space. We needed to find more burial sites—in a hurry."

Schammel said that the Board of Directors had already discussed expanding potential burial sites to areas located underneath golf courses, but couldn't get cooperation from the local owners. "Who wants to play a round of golf with a bunch of old people in suits hanging around the 9th green?" said Wedworth Wadsworth, Operations Manager at the prestigious Los Angeles Country Club. "We were very disappointed," said Schammel. "The Los Angeles Country Club seemed perfect for our purposes. We could have tucked granite niches and mausoleums within the trees lining the fairways and limited the flush ground stones to the areas circumnavigating the greens. The greens would have looked lovely with a constant supply of fresh cut flowers. And the sand traps would have been ideal for distributing loved ones' ashes. But, at the end of the day, LACC just wouldn't play ball with us."

Assuming that other golf courses located near Forest Lawn would take the same position, Forest Lawn went on to approach Universal Studios, Disneyland, Six Flags Magic Mountain, Knott's Berry Farm, Belmont Park, Fairytale Town, Great America, Legoland, Nut Tree Family Park, Pharaoh's Lost Kingdom, Rotary Storyland & Playland, Sea World and other popular southern California theme parks. "Many sitting on the Rose Bowl Board of Directors had problems integrating our memorial parks with race tracks and roller coasters." said Gordo, "So, ultimately, we ended up going with the Rose Bowl."

Refitting the Rose Bowl will begin during the summer of 2012. "We have quite a bit of work to do," said Chester "Squeak" Hardwick, Director of New Construction Operations. "Many of the families of people currently buried at Forest Lawn will inevitably want to have their loved ones exhumed and buried on the Rose Bowl playing field. Anticipating that, we're going to be offering several pricing tiers, depending on where they wish to be buried. Naturally, being buried on the 50-yard-line or in one of the end zones will come at a premium, but we'll have affordable re-burial packages available for everyone." When asked just how many graves the stadium will be able to accommodate, Hardwick wasn't sure. "It depends a lot on their current state of remains. We're planning on stacking graves 10-deep to maximize space and cut down on maintenance. We'll have to make sure that there is sufficient room between the lawn stones so that the grounds keepers can still cut the grass and stripe the playing field."

Another goal of the acquisition is to leave as much of the current stadium concourse design in tact, as possible. "While we will be expanding the concession stands to accommodate athletic fans and the addition of funeral goers, we're going to try to maintain the original flavor of the Rose Bowl that people have come to love over the years." said Hardwick. "In addition to beer and hot dogs, sports fans and funeral goers will be able to purchase bibles, artificial flowers, miniature coffin key rings, cremation jewelry, books of funeral songs, sympathy gifts, black baseball caps and T-shirts commemorating the special date they laid their loved one to rest."

"We'll also be building new wall crypts in quiet hallways between the restrooms and concession stands, while leaving room next to the press boxes for sarcophagi and columbaria. New mausoleums and cremation niches will be built alongside the new entrances, near the parking lots for easier hearse access.

So, how do the athletes feel about the new changes? "Personally, I think it's a nice improvement to what was already a classic venue," said Hamilton Winkworth, wide receiver for the USC Trojans. "I'll be able to make game-winning catches right on top of Uncle Ennis, so he can see all the action." Still, others aren't quite as excited. "The foot'n on the field is gonna be a mess," said Lamark Brown, offensive tackle for the

Trojans. "Havin' ta run in 'btween all dose granit haid markers iz gonna be impossible. Ah mean, ah cud break a damned ankle o sumpin'." The USC athletic department insists that the flat burial stones will not impede play. "We'll be outfitting all of the players with special rubber cleats designed for maximum traction on granite surfaces," said Steve Lupes, Senior Associate Athletic Director. "Sure, it will be a little tough taking a hit and landing on those grave markers, but our players will just have to learn how to suck it up."

This won't be the last marriage between corporate sponsorships and sporting venues. There's already been talk about the up and coming Pfizer Preparation H Championship Bowling Alley, the Stevie Wonder International Speedway, Roscoe's Chicken & Waffles Tennis Stadium, the Sonic Drive-In Bocce Ball Arena, the Jack Kevorkian Olympic Training Center and the Hell's Angels Oakland Memorial Stadium.

New Frontiers in Home Schooling

Boston, Massachusetts—Ever since Massachusetts issued the first compulsory education law in 1789, many parents have attempted to justify the reasons for home schooling their children: escalating violence in public schools, cutting down on gasoline for the SUV, freedom to teach religious beliefs, better quality of instruction, getting more yard work out of their kids and having someone around to fetch them beer. But, the parents of 15-year-old Ornice Bartimeus have chosen a more creative approach to educating their only son.

"We were concerned," said Adelia Bartimeus, Ornice's mother. "We wanted Ornice to experience all of the benefits of home schooling without sacrificing any of the important social aspects of attending a large public school." To do so, the Bartimeus' came up with a unique approach to making Ornice's experiences at home mirror those he would have at a public institution.

Like other children, Ornice's school day begins at 3:45 A.M. After donning his school uniform (a blue blazer over Orkin Termite Control overalls and rubber hip boots), he trundles downstairs for a hearty feast of waffles, chicken livers and grits. "After breakfast, I pack a bag full of his favorite treats and brush him out the door," says Adelia. "We make Ornice walk a half mile down County Road 109 in the rain to wait for the bus driven by Ornice's father, Bertram." As he approaches the bus, Bertram speeds away, making Ornice late for school.

Once Ornice arrives on campus, he just has time to sprint to the locker his father built for him behind the garage. "You're late, Bartimeus!" said his first period History teacher, Betram Bartimeus. "I suppose you're going to use that excuse about missing the bus again . . ."

After first period has ended, the Bartimeuses make Ornice jog in place outside for ten minutes to simulate walking to his next class. "We think it's important that Ornice has the same social interaction with others that public school students have," says Adelia. "So, we have him go outside and talk with Lyman Finwall, our 89-year-old neighbor. He can't hear and he has Alzheimer's, so it's a lot like talking to a Guidance Counselor."

During second period, Ornice's Math teacher (Bertram Bartimeus) asks the class to turn in their report cards that he sent home the day before. "Say, this signature looks like its been forged," said Bertram. "Oh, no sir . . . That's my father's signature alright. You can tell by the dippy way that he crosses his T's." Ornice and Bertram go around and around until Ornice is finally given two hours of detention for arguing with his teacher.

Third period is P.E., and because it's raining, Ornice trudges to the garage that his father has converted into a gymnasium, complete with the smell of old, sweaty socks, Ben Gay and decaying jock straps. "OK, Bartimeus," shouts Bertram. "You've got 5 minutes to get into your gym clothes. Today is calisthenics day!" Bertram puts young Ornice through his paces with a barrage of push-ups, sit-ups, wind sprints and four-count burpees. Because the calisthenics run overtime, Ornice has just 5-minutes to shower and change before he has to run into the kitchen for lunch.

Being Friday, the menu consists of fish sticks, macaroni and cheese and warm, orange Kool-aid. "Originally, I thought about serving Ornice healthy lunches—like the food I serve for dinner," says Adelia. "But, then I figured that would be setting Ornice up for failure later in life, so we decided to give him the same garbage that they serve at Ulysses S. Thonen High School. Bertram has even installed a vending machine outside filled with sugary soft drinks, candy, Twinkies, Cheetos and all of the other rubbish that they've banned from private schools."

Before lunch period ends, Ornice surreptitiously slips across the street with his next door neighbor Bobbie Kurban to engage in an age-old high school tradition: smoking cigarettes on the street corner while ogling girls. "Oh, sure. We know what Ornice is up to," says Bertram. "In fact, we encourage it. But just to make the experience as realistic as possible, I try to catch him in the act a couple of times a week to make him feel like he's doing something he's not supposed to. Once a month, I even take away his cigarettes and send him to the Principal's office."

Later on that afternoon, Ornice decides to ditch fifth period and goes out to cover the side of his neighbor's house with graffiti. "We knew that eventually he'd get around to defacing public property," says Bertram. "So, instead of making him walk all the way down to the Franklin Bridge underpass, we let him disfigure the neighbors' walls. They don't seem to mind. After all, it's normal thing to do for any full-blooded teenage, isn't it?"

During sixth period, Ornice is given permission to leave class to try out for the Chess Club, the Debating Society and the Lacrosse team. Because he's the only student trying out, he handily wins spots on all of the teams but fails to earn a spot in the Girls' Glee Club.

At 3:30, Ornice gathers up all of his books and heads out to catch the bus for home. On the way, he's cornered by a group of tough-looking thugs bent on stealing his money and giving him a wedgy. "Just because Ornice is schooled at home, we didn't want him to miss out on some of the more realistic aspects of becoming a young man," says Bertram. "So, three times a month, I hire his cousins to rough him up a bit, toss his homework into the gutter and give him a Dutch rub. It's good for him."

By the time he reaches home, Ornice is ready for some good news. "Ornice," said Adelia. "I have some wonderful news for you. Your Aunt Candalaria has agreed to be your date for the Senior Prom." Ornice could barely contain his elation at getting the news. His aunt had strung him along for over three weeks, and it was looking like he was going to miss the big event.

"We're all for home schooling," says Adelia. "But we're also glad that Ornice is learning the important lessons a young man his age needs. And, when he graduates, we've decided to continue his college education at home. In fact, Bertram has already started researching fraternity hazing."

The Great Soufflé Explosion

Lakehurst, New Jersey—Professional and amateur chefs around the world were stunned today after learning that Marion Pruss' lighter-than-air chocolate soufflé collapsed in flames, just as it was leaving the oven on the way to the dinner table. The dessert disintegrated before the family of 15 on the eve of the 74th anniversary of the infamous Hindenburg disaster—the German zeppelin that exploded into a fiery maelstrom—coincidentally, piloted by her grandfather, Capt. Max Pruss. Of the men, women and children in the house, all 15 were reported uninjured, but hungry. The only fatality reported was the soufflé, itself.

"I just don't know what happened," said Pruss. "We were all so excited; standing around the oven, waiting for the soufflé to complete its journey. Then, about three o'clock, the weather began changing—just as it left the oven, ascending for the table. As it slowly cleared the baking rack, the soufflé collapsed and burst into flames! Moments later, smoke started to fill the kitchen and the soufflé plunged to the ground taking my grandmother's dish with it. There were children screaming and running all around the kitchen while my husband Herb attempted to control the blaze with a garden hose. Honest to God. I could hardly breathe! I'm afraid I'm going to have to stop now. I'm feeling lightheaded and I think I'm losing my voice. I'm sorry . . ."

Soufflés have long been a staple of the Pruss' Sunday dinner, as they celebrated Max Pruss' escape from the Hindenburg, on May 6, 1937. "Chocolate soufflés were Max's favorite," said Marion. "Their onboard cook wasn't allowed to make lighter than air desserts because of the hydrogen onboard, so my grandmother tried to bake him one whenever he was home."

Grettel Willibrond, Marion Pruss' sister, remembers the afternoon well. "The dessert started out like any other soufflé. I preheated the oven to 400°, while Marion greased and lined the dish and began working on the ingredients," said Willibrond. "It looked like a perfect day for a soufflé—the sun was out, there were a few clouds in the sky. Nothing to indicate that trouble was in the air."

There have been a lot of theories as to what actually brought the soufflé down on what appeared to have been an otherwise routine day for baking. Witnesses to the explosion reported seeing blue discharges coming out of the oven—possibly from a gas leak or the accumulation of static electricity in the air.

Like the fateful Hindenburg, members of the family stated seeing flames shooting out of the port side of the dish and continued up the back of the oven until they developed into a giant mushroom cloud. Those in the kitchen remember hearing a muffled explosion, followed by large pieces of chocolate dessert hurtling through the air. "It's hard to say exactly what caused the explosion," said Helmet Lau, Jr., who is the son of the original Helmsman on the Hindenburg. "Although my brother Winfried was filming a home video at the time, he wasn't filming in the kitchen at the time of the explosion, so we'll never know."

Several days after the incident, while putting their kitchen back in order, Marion and Grettel notice fractures in the kitchen counter on both sides of the oven, indicating a huge amount of pressure originating from the dessert. "We think a crack might have developed in the outer skin of the soufflé dish that led to gas leaking into the oven," said Grettel. "And, since you're not supposed to open the oven door while cooking soufflés, no one knew anything was wrong."

"The destruction to the soufflé happened relatively quickly," said Manfred Wursted, Fire Chief for Battalion 27 in Lakehurst, New Jersey. "By my calculations, the entire incident took less than 37 seconds—about the same amount of time it took for the Hindenburg to come down. Using the same formula used in the original disaster by Addison Bain of NASA, flames covered the surface of the soufflé at a rate of 49 feet per second (15 meters/second)." Fortunately, Wursted was able to collect enough chocolate and porcelain fragments from the explosion to take back to his lab where his staff ran a sophisticated battery of tests."

Soufflé disasters such as the one that occurred in the Pruss' kitchen are no strangers to lighter-than-air cooking. According to Warak Ditinder, Chief Culinary Investigator for the State of New Jersey, "Lighter-than-air dessert explosions have occurred as a result of static electricity, lightning, oven failure, incendiary paint from the inside of the oven, punctures, structural failures in soufflé dishes and even sabotage," said Ditinder.

"Some suspect sabotage as the cause of the Pruss soufflé explosion," said Ditinder. "Marion's sister Evelyn was in town and wanted to bring dessert. But she is a terrible cook. Just terrible. Her desserts are so bad that they were used as land mines during the Normandy invasion of 1944," said Ditinder. "So, when she was told to bring mashed potatoes instead, she may have snuck into the kitchen and reset the oven timer so that the soufflé would overcook and explode. It's just a theory, though."

"What a lot of people don't know, is that this is not the first time a soufflé has exploded in a kitchen," said Ditinder. "The most famous explosion occurred in 1933 when a Navy cook was attempting to make 35 soufflés onboard the USS Akron, while being buffeted about at sea. That explosion was caused by a 19 year old kitchen apprentice, when he opened the oven door, attempting to taste a bit of the soufflé off of the top before it was done. It caused a massive explosion that spread through the depth charge compartment, ultimately sinking the Akron. Had it not been for the thick layer of chocolate on the surface of the water, the sailors might have starved to death before they were rescued. As it turned out, it also served as an effective shark repellent, so everyone onboard was saved."

Since that second fateful Lakehurst event, A. Hoehling Jr. published his version of the events, taken from the accounts of the survivors. "I've tightly reconstructed the timeline and reproduced the conditions, including time of day, ambient temperature and relative humidity," said Hoehling, Jr. "While there is still no concrete evidence to support it, I suspect that the soufflé exploded as a result of sabotage. All the evidence at this time points to the disgruntled Pruss sister."

The Tour De France Has a Female Winner!

Paris, France—Five years after the professional cycling world began allowing women to compete in the three month long Tour de France, the cycling world was stunned when a 21-year-old law student from Long Island, New York became the first woman in the 105-year history of the race to wear the coveted yellow jersey. But the victory did not come without controversy.

Flora Eloise Hobble, member of the Stay Free Mini-pad team won the 220 kilometer race in just over 12 weeks, literally destroying her male counterparts through a combination of arguments, temper tantrums and the silent treatment.

"I got off to a pretty shaky start," said Hobble. "My team director managed to misplace my custom made, carbon fiber makeup case on the flight over, so I had to send him out in search of a replacement. Fortunately, this being France and all, we were able to get one flown in from Paris, just minutes before the start of the first stage."

Three days prior to the race, six other women from four teams were disqualified for using banned breast implants. Although the disqualified cyclists claimed to have participated in rigorous wind tunnel tests, it was determined that the implants did not comply with strict International Cycling Union guidelines for aerodynamics and gave them an unfair advantage over their competitors—especially the men.

The integration of women into what has traditionally been an all-male athletic competition did not come easy. Many complained that including female competitors into the lineup would serve as an unnecessary distraction to the male riders. "I haven't seen my girlfriend for over two months," complained Jan Ullrich, captain of team Stanozolol. "And if you think its easy hiding sexual arousal in these skimpy, skin-tight cycling shorts, you'd better think again."

A number of course modifications were made to accommodate the female athletes. In past races, the three-week, 2200 kilometer race was punctuated by alternating stages of flat time trials and brutal mountain climbs with two rest days in between. To accommodate the female athletes, the race was shortened to 220 kilometers and extended to three months, so that the average ride is no longer than 1.8 kilometers a day. The two rest days were replaced with 15 shopping days.

This year's route was nearly identical to the 2006 course, except for the elimination of all of the hilly stages through the Pyrenees and the Alps and both the individual and team time trials. "A lot of the women athletes complained last year that the tour was just too damn hard," said Joseph-Marie-Arnaud Jaillet, Director of the Tour de France. "And quite frankly, I just couldn't put up with any more whining, so I caved in and shortened the course."

The first day began uneventfully with Hobble and her teammates taking an early lead. "To tell you the truth, I could have gone out a hell of a lot faster," said George Hincapie, member of team Discovery. "But I just couldn't pass up the opportunity to ride behind all of those beautiful lycra-clad butts." And in fact, that was the intent of the members of team Stay Free Mini-pad. "We knew that would get the guys," said Cheryl Simonelli, domestique to Flora Eloise Hobble. "And if that didn't work we were prepared to unzip our jerseys or remove them completely." Just such a move was pulled in 2009, which resulted in the disqualification of two women athletes from team Estee Lauder for exposing excess cleavage.

After a delayed start from Esch-sur-Alzette, the second week of competition finally got under way. "We didn't get out of town until almost noon," said Aaron Seraphim, sprinter for team Cofidis. "Dona Spunsler of team Midol wouldn't come out of her trailer. Someone said she was in there crying and refused to start the race." After further investigation, officials discovered that one of the other competitors made a disparaging remark that her butt looked "a little big" in her yellow shorts. "She took it pretty hard," said

Seraphim. "In fact, I heard a rumor that she's thinking about jumping ship at the end of this year's Tour to join the Quick Step team. They wear really cute dark blue shorts that make their athletes look slimmer."

A number of other changes have transpired since women have been allowed into the tour. Take for instance, the feed zones. "During the early years of the tour, we had to eat whatever they gave us as we flew through the feed zones; power bars, bananas, whatever," said Bob Roll, television commentator for this year's tour and husband of Harriett Binney, member of team Depo Provera. "But that's all changed. Now, most of the women have elected to get off their bikes for an hour and congregate at small sidewalk cafes, where they'll have tossed green salads with a low-fat vinaigrette dressing and a bottle of Evian water. Plenty of time is allowed for the female athletes to freshen up their makeup before getting back out onto the course."

Even the equipment has changed. While all of the cyclists in the tour still use some form of state of the art carbon fiber or aluminum frame, many of the bikes used by the female competitors now come equipped with additional features such as cell phone slots, Starbucks coffee mug holders and large mirrors for those quick mascara touch-ups.

As the fourth week of the race ended, a number of riders were involved in a horrific crash with just 100 meters to go to the finish in Cambo-les-Bains. Elinor Neugebauer from team Vagisil was reaching down for her water bottle and broke two of her nails. When she abruptly stopped in the middle of the peloton to examine the damage, she caused 34 of her fellow competitors to crash. The carnage was the worst ever recorded in the history of the Tour.

"While a number of athletes with broken collar bones, dislocated fingers and severe road rash brushed themselves off and continued the race," said Roll, "Neugebauer's injuries were deemed much more serious. She was transported off the course by a Flight for Life helicopter and taken to a local manicurist." A specialist in acrylic nails was being flown in from the United States. "We won't know until later tonight if they'll be able to repair those two nails or if she'll even be able to resume racing tomorrow."

During the final day of the race, the peloton had to face some of its most grueling terrain: the designer stores on the Champs Elysee. "We did pretty well when we were out in the countryside," said Noemi Nastasi from team DivaCup. "Cruising past all of those farmers and young French boys without any shirts was pretty easy. But when Chandra Goldsby saw that Prada boutique, I knew we were going to lose her." One by one, as the women passed Sephora, Armani and Gucci, the field began to thin out. By the time the remainder of the peloton cruised into the finish there were only two women cyclists left: Hobble and her domestique, Twana Kruszewski.

"It was a thrilling experience. One that I'll never forget," said Hobble. When asked what her plans were after winning the most prestigious bicycle race in the world, she said, "Well, first off, I'm going go home and get a pedicure. Maybe have a few of the girls by for a sleepover and a pillow fight. Then it's back to school. I've got some Civil Procedure and Torts to catch up on."

Fly Me To The Snooze

Washington, D.C.—The Federal Aviation Administration announced sweeping new changes today to eliminate the wave of sleeping air traffic controllers at major airports throughout the country. The most recent incident occurred at the Reno-Tahoe International Airport, where a controller snoozed through a pilot's urgent plea to land his aircraft with a sick passenger. By the time the controller woke up, the aircraft had already safely landed, unloaded its passengers, sent four pallets of luggage to Cleveland, had the interior cabin space detailed, completed a scheduled maintenance, stocked the kitchens, washed the exterior of the plane, loaded a full compliment of passengers bound for Taipei and took off.

"We're absolutely incensed over the problem of sleeping air controllers," said Federal Aviation Administrator Randy Babbitt. "We intend to get to the bottom of this problem and come up with solutions that are fair to both the air controllers and the flying public."

The main problem air traffic controllers contend with is so much down time in between flights coupled with long shifts. That's what happened to Deepfar Praam who fell asleep during his midnight shift at the Corpus Christi/Kingsville International Airport in Corpus Christi, Texas. "We're supposed to sit in this stuffy room all by ourselves, looking into the dark, while trying to come up with ways to stay awake. Then, without any warning, an inebriated pilot from an approaching aircraft requests landing instructions," says Praam. "I mean, c'mon . . . between coming to and trying to interpret his slurring words, it's damn near impossible to keep it together."

One of the solutions Babbitt was talking about is completely redesigning the working environment of air traffic controllers. At the current time, controllers are forced to work in close, cramped quarters at the top of control towers or down in stuffy radar centers. The space is usually dimly lit so that controllers can simultaneously scan radar screens, porn sites, widescreen televisions, pay per view movies and various forms of electronic equipment while listening to their cell phones and iPods. "That's one of the problems," complained Leo Helmholtz, air traffic controller at Eppley Field in Omaha, Nebraska. "The controllers are just overwhelmed with technology. After the first 45 minutes, our brains are fried, so we just go to sleep."

To get to the bottom of the problem, the FAA will be implementing a number of bold solutions, beginning on January 1, 2012. The first steps will be to remove all of the chairs behind the consoles and completely eliminate restroom breaks. "We feel that if we can keep the controllers standing throughout their shifts, worrying about their bladders, they're a lot less likely to fall asleep," said Giorgio Basso, an Italian Human Resources specialist on loan from Alitalia Airlines.

Another ingenious technique Basso has tried is replacing traditional work desks and chairs with mini-treadmills. "Each controller's workstation will be human powered. As long as the controller maintains a walking speed of at least 4 mph, their radar screens will continue to function normally. If they slow down, everything goes dark. It will not only keep them awake, but fit as well."

This isn't the first time that human power has been used to keep workers alert. "We used the same concept for the swing shift at Three Mile Island and Chernoble nuclear power stations, but of course, that was before we had perfected our protocols. Everything's different now."

Besides running, FAA authorities are looking at other ways to integrate fitness into the controllers' routine. "We've recognized that one of the reasons why controllers are falling asleep on the job is because they're overweight and out of shape," says Tami Bellefontaine, head trainer at Harbodies Gym in Port Arthur, Texas. "We're going to start introducing an incentive program for controllers who successfully jump rope, jog in place, lift weights, workout to Richard Simmons tapes and learn to ride pogo sticks," says Bellefontaine. "The entire program is part of a study being underwritten by the American College of Sports Medicine in

Indianapolis, Indiana which will present their findings at their annual meeting in 2014. At the end of this year, we're going to hold a lavish awards banquet called 'Aviation's Biggest Losers,' and dole out wonderful prizes to the controllers who were not only able to stay awake the longest, but also lost the most weight."

Of course, not every air traffic controller will likely respond to such positive direction. For those requiring extra supervision, the FAA is prepared to take harsher measures to protect their expensive assets. "One idea that's been tossed around is to bring in retired nuns from local Catholic schools," said Viktor Efimov, head of the FAA's Special Programming Department. "Anyone who's ever attended Catholic school will tell you that there are no stricter task masters than nuns."

"We've developed something special for those naughty air traffic controllers," says Sister Aida Agnes Rudegristle. "The first time they're caught dozing, we'll make them write on a blackboard, 'I will not let the airplanes crash,' 1,000 times. If they're caught sleeping while on duty a second time, then we'll rap them on their knuckles with a ruler. Third offenses will result in controllers having to kneel during their entire shift," says Sister Rudegristle. "We think that eventually, they'll straighten up."

Another method that's being considered is electric pulse therapy. Beginning next month, air traffic controllers manning the towers in Shreveport, Louisiana will start wearing electronic "dog collars" that emit an ear-piercing scream if the collar senses that the controller is beginning to slump forward. It will also send an announcement throughout the airport's public address system in all of the terminals, "Warning! Warning! An air traffic controller is falling asleep!" Of course, all of the controllers will have to avoid bending over to pick up items off of the floor, tie their shoes or eating their lunch while wearing the collars.

If all of the previously mentioned methods fail to keep the controllers awake during their shifts, the FAA is prepared to offer a medical solution—black market drugs. "We've been studying the American trucking industry for years," says Pierre Thibodaux, M.D. from the world famous Sleep Disorder Clinic in Legard, France. "After a number of futile attempts at behavior modification, the International Teamsters Union finally threw in the towel and started letting truckers load up on caffeine, nicotine, amphetamines, Ecstasy, cocaine, Ritalin, Ampakines and even Yohimbine. Anything goes. As long as it keeps them awake."

"It's obvious that we have a real problem here," says Babbitt. "But we feel that we've contracted with some of the best specialists in the world and we're on our way to some pretty exciting solutions. We just ask the American public not to be too hard on our brave men and women who spend their lives in the dark."

Malcolm Brown, M.D.—Ghetto Doctor

Malibu, California—In an effort to redeem himself after his embarrassing DUI arrest, the Academy Award winning director, Mel Gibson, is poised to release two new film projects: "Ghetto," written entirely in Ebonics and its sequel, "Malcolm Brown, M.D.," scripted entirely in Pig Latin.

Gibson, famous for producing other films like "The Passion of the Christ" and "Apocolypto," that were made using the Aramaic and Yucatec Mayan languages, said the two new films promise to be a more accurate reflection of the true emotions that surround life in a low-income, high-crime housing neighborhood of Michigan.

"Ghetto' will be filmed entirely on location at the Foster Chubbs housing project in southern Detroit," said Gibson. "In the past, most films that feature well-known black actors failed to communicate the passion and conflict of the day to day challenges of living in destitute, crime-ridden surroundings. The audience finds it hard to believe the words of a well known actor when they sound like they've just graduated from Harvard."

Gibson gave us a sneak peek at the scripts, based on the early drafts of the award winning screenplays by Stuart Eisenbarth:

The scene opens with Malcolm, the younger brother of Tyrone Munsell Brown who's currently doing time in Sing Sing for impersonating a transvestite, arguing with his sick mother about his future:

Malcolm: Mornin', Mama. How iz ya feeling dis here morning? Did ya gots uh pimp-tight nights sleep and shit?

Mama: Oh, ya know. I never can seem ta git mo' than uh couple o' hours o' rack tyme. The rest o' da tyme, I just toss an' turn, listening ta all o' da po-po sirens.

Malcolm: Do ya wants anthin fo' breakfast? Is ya hungry? Don't make me come ovah there bitch . . .

Mama: Oh, nahh thanks, Malcolm. My stomach'stoo upset ta eat anythin' dis here morning. I th'o't muh ma jive cancer iz kicking up ag'in. But, ya jet ahead an' sit down. I'll make ya som eggs. What tyme iz ya going ta skoo taday?

Malcolm: I'm not goin ta skoo taday, Mama. I'm going ta visit Tyrone, then I'm going ta jet ta da park ta see if I can sell som drugs. We really need da damn money, bitch.

Mama: Oh, Malcom. You know how much ah trip about ya when you out in da park alone. Why don' ya git uh tight job like yo' boy, Washington?

Malcolm: But Washington iz uh pimp, Mama. That's nahh kind o' life. True, dere iz uh lot o' fringe benefits an' all, but he has ta werk honky hours. I an' I don' like da kind o' gear dat he's always wearing. Ya'll is mad stupid.

Mama: I know, homey. But I'd just feel uh little bettah if ya could start making some real dough an' meet some nice ho's. Maybe settle down an' raise uh family an' all . . .

"Malcolm Brown, M.D.," is the compelling sequel to "Ghetto" and follows Malcolm as he struggles through college, finally graduating from Jackson Koppenhaver Medical School, becoming the first college educated member of the Brown family. Gibson elected to tell the entire story in Pig Latin " . . . because it's the universal language," said Gibson. "Whether you're from San Francisco, Mexico City or New Delhi, India, every kid has grown up mangling their native language using Pig Latin.

In the opening scene, Malcolm is on his third day on grand rounds at Rochelle Sheckleheise Memorial Medical Center. Moises Dyckman, the

Chief of Surgery, confronts the new Dr. Brown about a patient on the floor:

Dr. Dyckman: Ellway, Dr. Ownbray, ethay atientpay inksthay ehay isyay avinghay ayay earthay attackyay. Atwhay isyay youray iagnosisday?

Malcolm: Ellway, Dr. Yckmanday, Iyay inkthay e'shay ootay youngay otay ebay avinghay ayay earthay attackyay.

Dr. Dyckman: Youay aymay ebay ightray. Utbay idday youay owknay atthay ethay atientpay omescay omfray ayay amilyfay ofyay ansvestitestray?

Malcolm: Iyay asn'tway awareyay ofyay atthay. Erethay areyay onay otesnay otay atthay effectyay inyay ethay atient'spay ecordsray.

Dr. Dyckman: Youay ustmay earnlay otay expectyay ethay unexpectedyay ymay earday dray. Ownbray. You'llay earnlay . . .

"I think it's easy to see why I chose that language," said Gibson. "It's like you're standing right there in the Intensive Care unit."

After the completion of these two films, Gibson said that he's going to continue to explore other subject matter using their native languages. "My next film is going to be about the 1995 tragedy on Mount Everest, told entirely in Sharwa, the native language of the Sherpas of Nepal. After that, I'm going to do a remake of "The King and I" done in Siamese with fifteen sets of subtitles. It's going to be my first foreign language musical."

The Vatican III: New Changes for Roman Catholics

Vatican City, Italy—On the fifth anniversary of the election of John Ratzinger, Pope Benedict XVI, the Vatican announced today that they have concluded proceedings of the Vatican III. Not since the second Ecumenical Council adjourned in 1965 has the Catholic Church adopted such sweeping changes in doctrine, aimed at reclaiming many of its lost parishioners.

"When Pope John Paul died in 2005, we decided to seize the opportunity to spruce things up a bit," said Joaquin Navarro-Valls, Vatican spokesman. "To tell you the truth, most of the College of Cardinals felt that John Paul was kind of stodgy. He needed to get out a bit more and live a little. We couldn't wait to get some new blood into the leadership of the church."

One of the first things that the council agreed upon after his death was a radical change in the matrimonial laws for priests. "We're losing priests left and right," said Cardinal Jorge Mario Bergoglio, Archbishop of Buenos Aires. "As of today, priests are not only free to marry, they're encouraged. And we're even going one step further." He's referring, of course, to the church's decision to adopt the practice of polygamy; the very same practice abandoned by the Mormon Church over 100 years ago. "No reflection on the Mormons, but they just didn't know how to handle their women," said Bergoglio. "We've established a whole new set of guidelines for young priests that will keep them engaged every minute of the day. They'll be so busy chasing after their twelve young wives, they won't have time to even look at little boys."

New changes have been planned for the 94,000 American nuns, as well. "Just about anyone who's ever been dragged off to Sunday school can remember how difficult it was to learn with those stern old nuns in their starched black habits leaning over you, threatening to whack you over the knuckles with a ruler," said George Carey the Archbishop of Canterbury. "Now, we're allowing nuns to go ahead and start wearing civilian clothes. In fact, I just saw Sister Maria Theresa Rabinowitz in a very hot mini-skirt and a low-cut Hooters halter top. Class attendance is way, way up and they're much more comfortable."

A big change with Vatican II was the shift from Latin to English while conducting Mass. Many English speaking Catholics struggled to understand Latin. With Vatican III, parishioners will experience yet, another change. Since the federal government gave up trying to suppress the illegal flow of immigrants across the U.S. border from Mexico, practicing Catholics are right back in the same boat again. According to Church sources, "The only people going to Mass are the illegal immigrants and they can't understand a word of English." As a result, the Vatican decided to concede by making Spanish the official language spoken in all services. "What the hell," said Navarro-Valls, "They're the only ones who go to church anyway. We might as well make it easy for them."

The College of Cardinals has also been concerned with the world-wide attrition of practicing lay Catholics. "In this day and age, people just don't have time to go to confession, say their penance, attend Mass, go to soccer practice and pick up the kids from their music lessons. They're just too damned busy," said Cardinal Avery Dulles, leader of the Catholic Doctrine of Faith. "So, we think we've come up with a solution." Beginning next year, the Vatican will begin building drive-through chapels. Open 24 hours a day, seven days a week, the "Pray & Go's" will let busy families drive up to a take-out window, confess their sins together, receive penance, get a complimentary rosary and a DVD of this Sunday's Mass. All for $14.95. Holy Communion is $10 extra.

Prior to Vatican II, many practicing Catholics found it difficult to abstain from eating meat on Fridays. Vatican II changed all that and allowed parishioners to anything they wanted on Fridays. "We always felt that abstinence from meat was a harsh directive," said Cardinal Dulles. "Even I had problems enjoying a ball game on Fridays with all of those hot dogs around." Meatless Fridays also took a severe toll on the meatpacking business. "We were really hurting there for a while," said Big Ed Newton, owner of K & B Meatpackers and one of the Catholic Church's largest benefactors. "Those damn rules were killing our sales with all of that no meat business. Thank God that's over!"

Not only are Catholics allowed to eat meat on Fridays now, with Vatican III, they're actually required to. "Parishioners must eat meat in at least one meal; more if they can," said Dulles. "And vegetarians aren't exempt either. If they can't face up to a good steak or meatball sub, then they can eat anything that's deep-fried in animal fat."

Even the sacraments have changed with Vatican III. "The Eucharist has traditionally been offered in the form of unleavened bread," said Cardinal Bergoglio. "But, that's just become too much of a hassle. Besides, with the nuns' liberation, we can't find anyone to make them anymore. So, instead, we're starting to pass out chocolate M & Ms at the alter. They're cheaper, easier to find, gentler on the digestive tract and parishioners can just reach into the bag and grab a handful themselves without all of the pomp and circumstance. It's also made people want to receive Holy Communion again." The Church has also done completely away with fasting prior to the sacraments. "With all of the eating disorders in teenage girls these days, we just didn't want anyone pointing the finger at us."

There have been a number of other changes aimed at helping parishioners get through their busy day. Says Cardinal Dulles, "For parishioners who regularly attend Mass, we're issuing special punch cards. After twelve masses, they get to take one Sunday off. And, by eliminating the Epistle, the Gospel, the Sermon and the Canon we've been able to shave off over 40-minutes from the length of the Mass. We feel that if people really want to hear all that, they can get them on the Church Channel or the Internet."

"All in all, we think that these are going to be positive changes for modern practicing Catholics," said Cardinal Bergoglio. "We need to dispense with all of this historical falderal get back to basics."

Also by Allen Smith
Ski Instructors Confidential–The stories ski instructors
swap back at the lodge

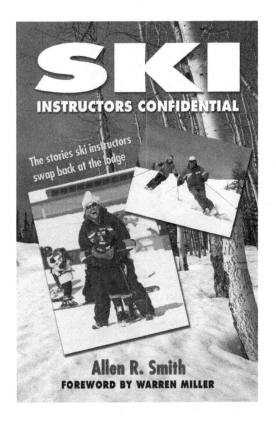

Available at all major booksellers or at www.snowwriter.com